CW01333649

THE ESSENCE OF KARATE

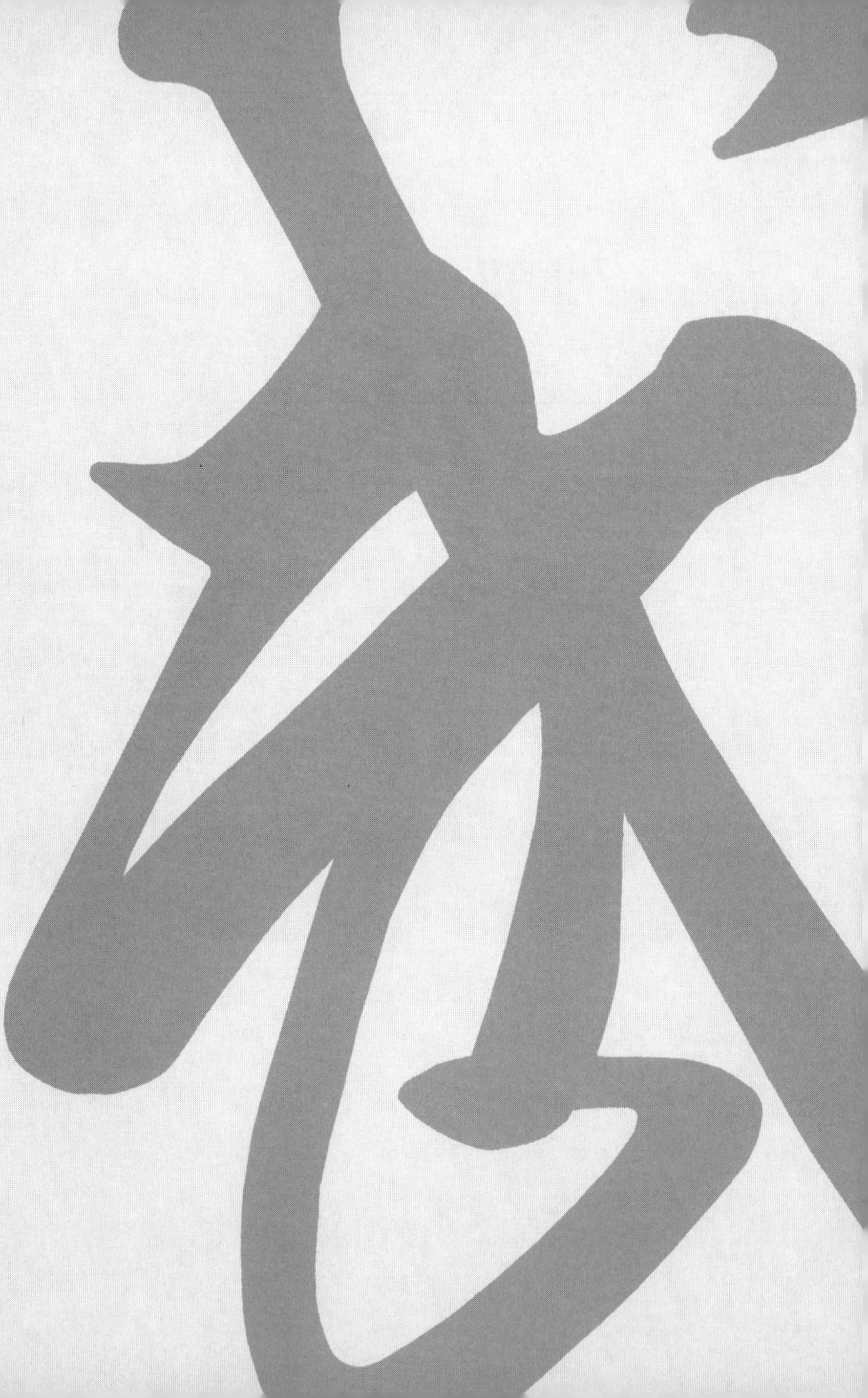

The Essence of
KARATE

Gichin Funakoshi

FOREWORD BY Hirokazu Kanazawa
AFTERWORD BY Gisho Funakoshi

TRANSLATED BY Richard Berger

KODANSHA INTERNATIONAL
Tokyo · New York · London

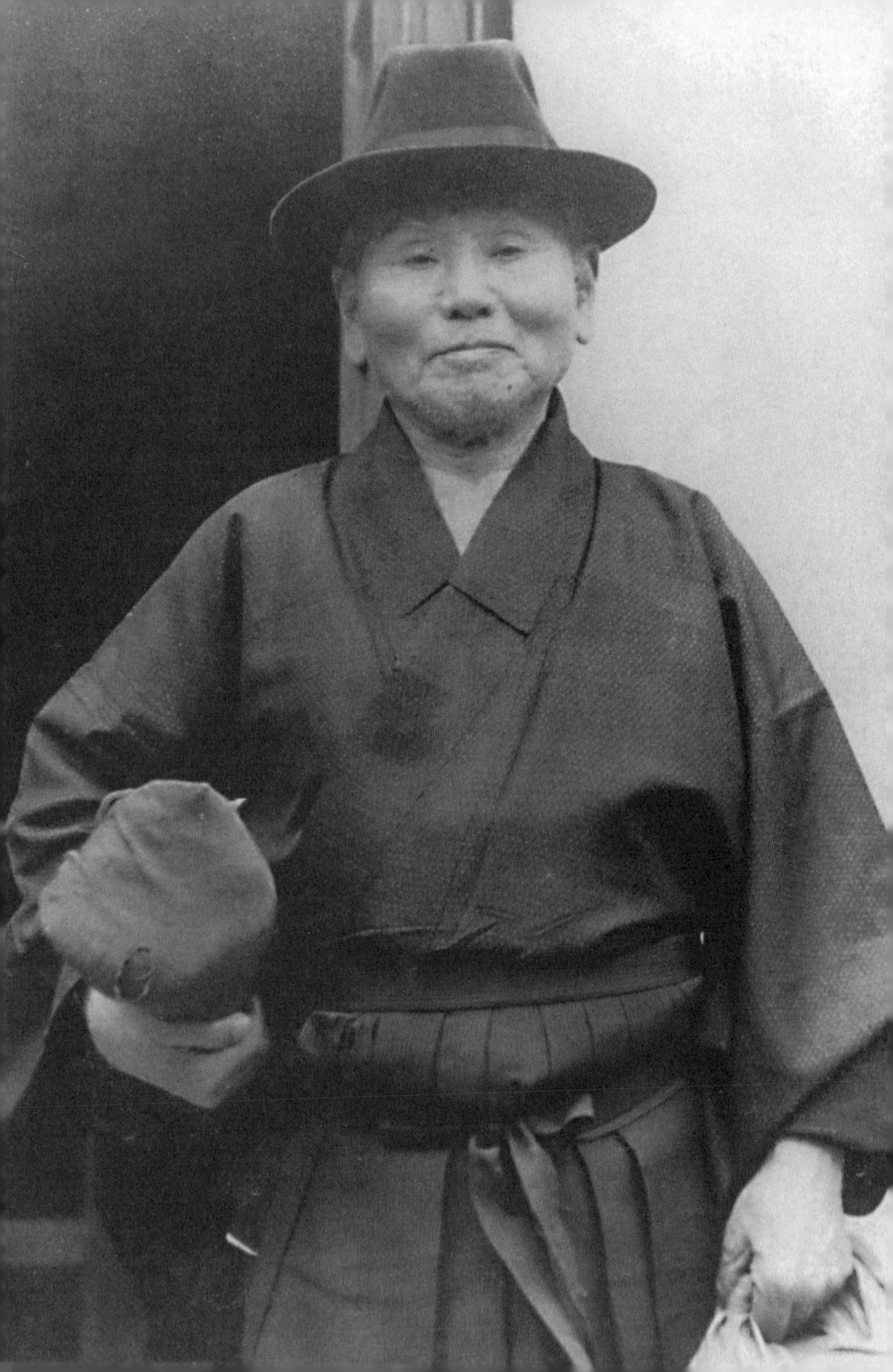

Gichin Funakoshi standing in his garden.

FACING PAGE: Master Funakoshi usually wore a *hakama* skirt and put on *geta*, wooden clogs, when he went out.

ABOVE: Master Funakoshi dressed in formal Japanese wear.

BELOW: At his home around 1930.

ABOVE: In his study in 1957.

BELOW: Writing Japanese calligraphy by request at Toyama in 1952.

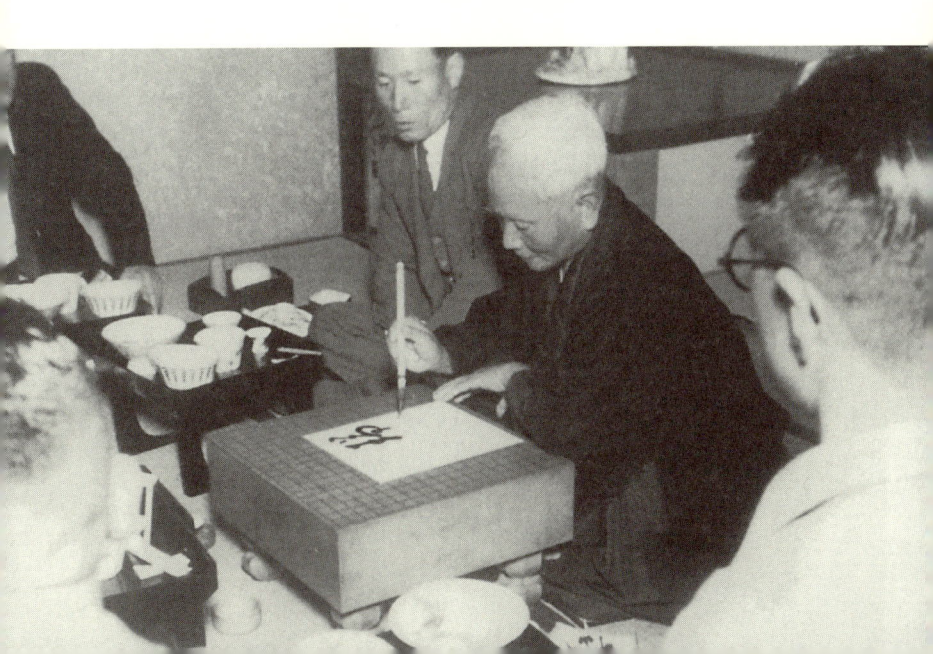

Instruction at the Meisei Juku in Koishikawa, Tokyo, around 1925.

FACING PAGE: Master Funakoshi blocks a stick attack with the weapon known in the Okinawan dialect as a *sai*, at the Keio University dojo around 1930.

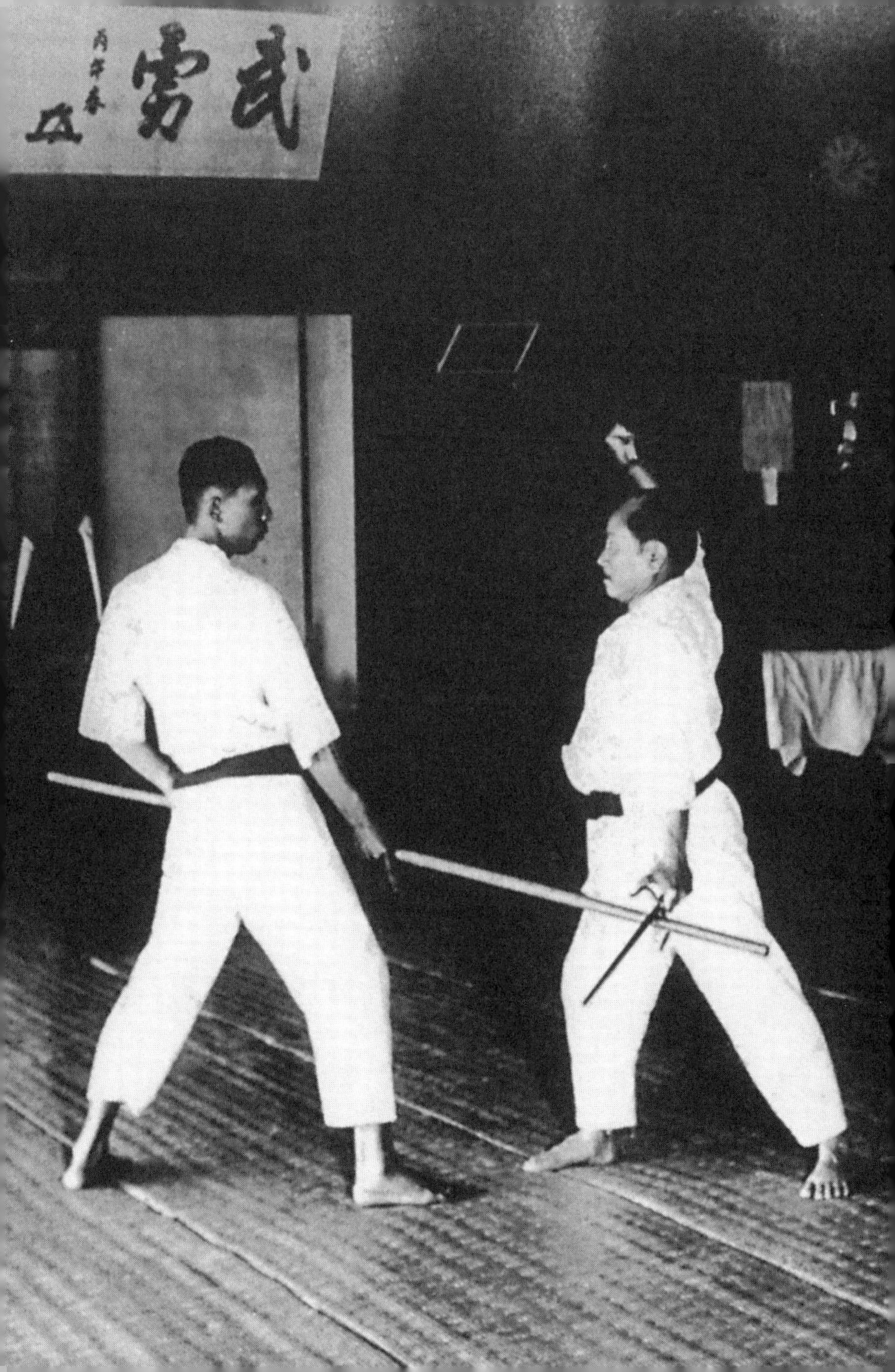
武勇

Notes from the Publisher
The use of macron to denote Japanese long vowels has been employed only in cases where the word or name is relatively unknown in the West. For Japanese words and names in common usage (e.g., Tokyo, Shotokan, karate-do) the macron has been omitted.

The names of modern and contemporary Japanese appear in the Western order, while those of historical figures (pre-1868) are written in the traditional order: surname preceding given name.

Edited in cooperation with Musashi Editorial Ltd.

Distributed in the United States by Kodansha America LLC, and in the United Kingdom and continental Europe by Kodansha Europe Ltd.

Published by Kodansha International Ltd., 17–14 Otowa 1-chome, Bunkyo-ku, Tokyo 112–8652.

English translation 2010 by Richard Berger.
All rights reserved. Printed in Japan.
ISBN 978-4-7700-3118-1

First edition, 2010
18 17 16 15 14 13 12 11 10   10 9 8 7 6 5 4 3 2 1

Library of Congress Cataloging-in-Publication Data is available

www.kodansha-intl.com

CONTENTS

FOREWORD BY Hirokazu Kanazawa		13
A Story of Karate	I	25
	II	31
	III	37
	IV	47
	V	55
	VI	63
	VII	71
	VIII	77
	IX	83
	X	91
	XI	99
AFTERWORD BY Gisho Funakoshi		105
NOTES		123

FOREWORD
Memories of Master Gichin Funakoshi

More than fifty years have passed since the death of Master Gichin Funakoshi, who is recognized as the "Father of Modern Karate." Today, karate, after having spread far and wide across the world, has become a universal language and was even featured as the theme for a synchronized swimming routine in Olympic competition.

This can be credited to Master Gichin Funakoshi's journey from Okinawa to Tokyo in 1922 to take part in the First Annual Athletic Exhibition, hosted by Japan's Ministry of Education, to give a karate demonstration. After this he remained in Tokyo, spreading karate through his instruction, mainly to university students.

Until that time, Sensei Funakoshi had been active in spreading karate not just among a select number of people, but as a Japanese martial art, a form of physical education intended for everyone, with the central aim of cultivating individuals of character. It is for this reason more than any other that Master Funakoshi is recognized as the Father of Modern Karate.

I had the honor of studying under Sensei Funakoshi from the time that I joined the karate team at Takushoku University until the last years of his life.

Postwar Japan, eager to rebuild itself into a new nation, was brimming with activity. The same also held true for the world of karate at the time. During the war, university students had been mobilized for the war effort and all team activities had been halted. After the war ended, however, a flood of university karate teams appeared again. With the start of the [Japanese] school year in April, I, along with the rest of my first-year classmates, hurried to join the karate team in our school and our numbers were so great that we were not all able to fit into the dojo [training hall].

I and the other first-year students lived in accordance

with the teachings of Sensei Funakoshi when he told us: "Do not think that karate is just for the dojo," and "Apply karate to all things." Taking this advice to heart, we all reached an agreement: Should any of us let our guard down while waiting on the platform for a train, one of the others would be allowed to strike from the shadows. If anyone should be caught unawares while drinking tea, then the rest were encouraged to attack from behind.

One topic that we constantly discussed concerned the mysterious nature of Sensei Gichin Funakoshi. While we had all heard stories of his heroic exploits in his youth, there remained a simple question that we could not help but ask ourselves: We hear about how incredible Sensei Funakoshi is, but is he still strong even now?

At the time, Sensei Funakoshi taught karate at several universities in Tokyo, including Takushoku University. When he traveled, a university student was assigned to accompany him on his journeys and I, as a first-year student, was given the honor, albeit stressful, of fulfilling this important role.

Sensei Funakoshi had glowing skin and radiant features; when he emerged from his home the surrounding area would suddenly brighten with his good cheer. Dressed in a kimono, he always maintained good posture and, wearing tall wooden clogs and sporting a hat, always conveyed a tidy appearance and an air of dignity.

One day, sitting beside Sensei Funakoshi in the taxi as I escorted him to his next destination, a thought crossed my mind: Now that he is eighty years old, I wonder if the Master is really as strong as he was in his heroic youth. What would happen now if I were to try something against Sensei Funakoshi? It was at that very instant that I heard him say, "Kanazawa-san, what were you just thinking?"

"Nothing," I said in a fluster. "Nothing at all." I realized that he had just read my mind.

There was another similar incident, while I was once practicing the kata Kankū Dai. Sensei Funakoshi came over to me and said, "Kanazawa-san, you should spread your feet farther apart and lower your hips." "Yes, sir," I said in response, but was confused because I had performed the movement just as he had shown us. Then the Master spoke again: "Kanazawa-san, I am an old man of eighty; I cannot do this. But you are young, and youth is the time to strengthen your body. That is why you should lower your hips."

Once again he had read my mind, realizing what I had been thinking the moment the thought had occurred to me. It was then that any doubts or other irrational notions I had ever had about the Master disappeared completely.

Sensei Funakoshi was a gracious educator, calligrapher, and man of culture. I understand that he began training in karate not to become a martial artist, but because he had been frail as a child and wished to strengthen his body, believing that karate would provide him with the means to do so. By chance, one of his classmates at school was the son of karate master Azato Yasutsune. Before long, Sensei Azato decided that, rather than teach his own son, it would be better to send him to train under Sensei Itosu Yasutsune. And Funakoshi, as a schoolmate, was given the opportunity to accompany Sensei Azato's son in the training.

The expression of Sensei Azato's teaching methods was the exact opposite of that of Sensei Itosu, and I sensed that it was this experience that provided the basis for Sensei Funakoshi's broadmindedness. Although their methods were different, the objective was the same. Both of these instructors were also said to have been prone to illness in their childhoods. And yet these masters elevated their weaknesses to the highest levels of strength.

Sensei Azato and Sensei Itosu's instructor was Master Matsumura Sōkon, a legendary figure [in the world of Okinawan karate].

While in his fifties, Sensei Funakoshi, who had been a schoolteacher in Okinawa from his early twenties, was invited to Tokyo as a representative of Okinawa to demonstrate karate at the First Annual Athletic Exhibition. Following the demonstration he received requests for karate lessons and, despite a lack of economic backing, stayed in

Tokyo, where he remained to live out the rest of his life.

At that time in Japan people in their fifties usually lived in retirement. Yet Sensei Funakoshi, fully understanding that he could expect to face many difficulties, took up a new life living in a student dormitory. While he had been reduced to living in a state of abject poverty, I heard that he took his meager circumstances in his stride. Discarding all concern for himself, he was truly living a life of service to others.

In his sixties, he began to write more and also to discuss the subject of advancing in age.

The three masters Matsumura, Azato, and Itosu had all suffered from poor health when they were young and began training in karate as a means to overcome their conditions. Sensei Funakoshi, seeing these masters live long lives into their eighties and nineties, went on to write the following, which can be found in the pages of this book:

> Karate came about to prevent the decline of the spirit and atrophying of physical strength.

While it is easy to fall prey to delusions of our youth, as we get older, we are not so easily deceived. As such, because we are better able to see the movement of an opponent's hands and our bodies feel lighter and move with greater freedom, we are able to polish our techniques.

When he reached his seventies, the hardship that Sensei Funakoshi had endured up to that time was rewarded with the construction by his students of the Shotokan (Shoto Hall) dojo in the Zōshigaya area of Tokyo's Toshima Ward. The building, which bore Funakoshi's nom de plume "Shoto," was a source of joy for the Master as well as his students.

That dojo, however, was destroyed in the Great Tokyo Air Raid [of March 10, 1945] and, in a further blow, Funakoshi lost his son Yoshitaka to illness the same year. Yoshitaka, who was commonly known as Gigo, possessed karate skills and character that were of the highest caliber, and had been viewed as the Master's likely successor. Around this time, Funakoshi also suffered the loss of many of his students, who died in battle after being called to war. In later years, family members of these students would recall that Sensei Funakoshi, upon hearing of their deaths, had traveled out to the countryside to attend their funerals.

When he reached his eighties, peace had returned to Japan and Funakoshi resumed teaching, mainly to university students.

It was around this time in his life that I first met the Master. Although it was after he had lost everything while in his seventies, he was an individual who, as described in this book which he wrote in his sixties, "embodied the ideal of mind and body." There was an air of mystery about the man and he was someone who we all looked up to with admiration.

Sensei Masatomo Takagi [who later became administrative director of the Japan Karate Association] and others decided to build a new dojo for Sensei Funakoshi, which opened in 1956 in the Yotsuya district of Tokyo. That dojo was made the headquarters of the Japan Karate

Association, which I entered that year as a member of the first class of instructor trainees. Although Sensei Funakoshi no longer put on a karate uniform or provided direct instruction, he would often spend his time contentedly watching us train. It was in the following year that the Master passed away peacefully.

Sensei Funakoshi set an example by always being ready to start new endeavors, radiating a sense of dignity from within, even in the face of hardship. He taught me just how big a person could be.

As I approach my eighties, I now find myself thinking again about the way Sensei Funakoshi lived.

As an educator, compared with Sensei Funakoshi, one thing that I believe I could never hope to match is his ability to continually draw out the very best from his students, even without uttering a single word.

His students viewed their teacher with awe, revered and studied him and, in the process, were able to find themselves among good companions brimming with ambition.

Also, the senior students looked after the juniors while the junior students respected their seniors. Through such vertical connections, along with the horizontal connection of friends learning from one another, Sensei Funakoshi demonstrated how such wonderful relationships could lead to the weaving of a rich human community.

Additionally, Sensei Funakoshi always maintained a cool distance, never allowing anything to bother him, yet displayed dignity and was an internationally minded person as well as a gentleman.

I learned from the Master that, with only a toothbrush and a karate uniform, I could live anywhere. He did not teach this to me through words; it was watching Sensei Funakoshi that made me realize that I wanted to be like him, and set in motion the life that I have led.

I was in my twenties when I began teaching karate overseas and, while I experienced financial difficulties, I never once felt as though I was enduring hardship. Regardless of our circumstances, we never viewed it as stress, but decided instead it would be best to enjoy the situation. Put another way, regardless of one's circumstances, with ingenuity, there is always a way.

Because I am eager for many people to have the strong courage to embrace the realization "I can do it too," it is my wish to set an example for all, which is why I set out anew to live each and every day through the end of my life.

As the writing of these words happens to coincide with the recession that has struck the global economy, it is my heartfelt wish that the readers of this book, no matter what circumstances they may find themselves in, be proud-minded warriors with spiritual richness and dignity, and internationally minded individuals who wish for the happiness of their companions around the world.

And I call on these people to cultivate this spirit and pass it on to the next generation. This is the ideal to which I aspire, the ideal that I focus on achieving every day.

Hirokazu Kanazawa
PRESIDENT, shotokan karate-do international federation

A STORY OF KARATE

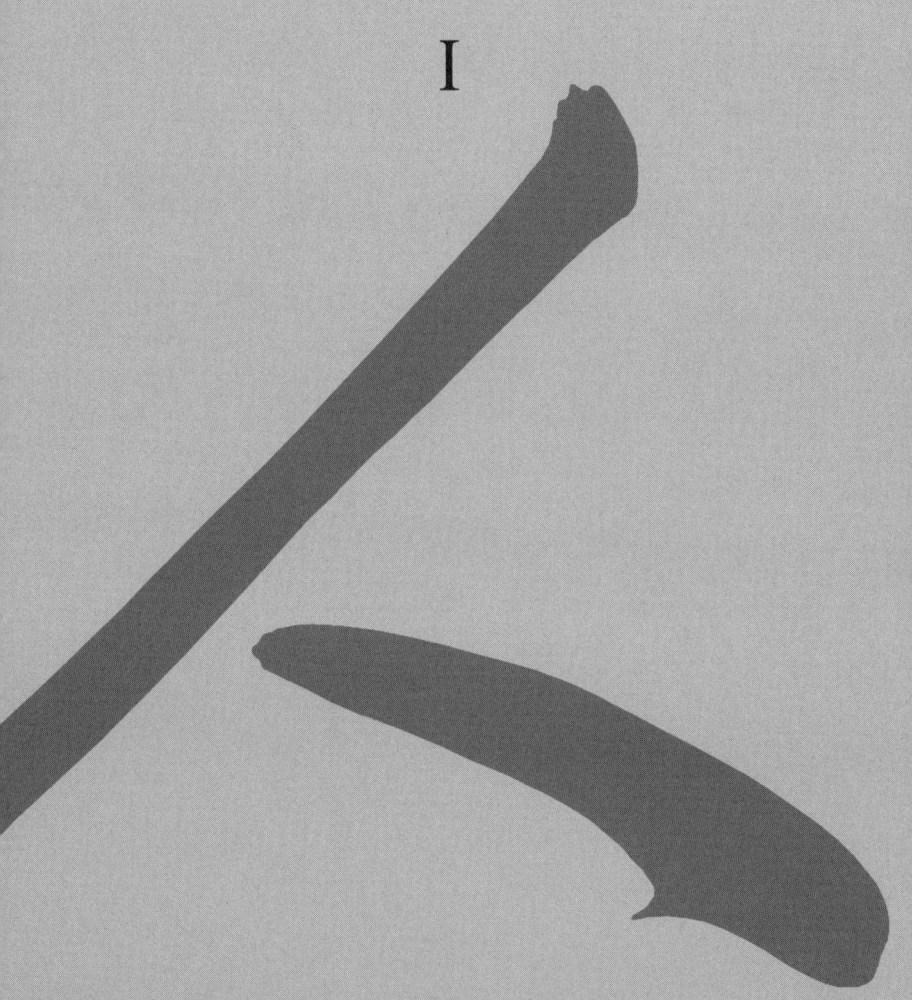

I

Karate is said to have begun with Bodhidharma.[1]

Bodhidharma traveled from faraway India to the lands of the Liang Dynasty [in China], an extremely arduous journey involving the crossing of towering mountains, dark valleys, and mighty rivers. It was there that he lectured Emperor Wu of Liang [about Buddhism] and, approximately 1,400 years ago, during the Northern Wei Dynasty, spent nine years gazing at a wall [in meditation] at a Shaolin monastery in Henan Province.

After his death, Bodhidharma is said to have been buried at the foot of Bear Ear Mountain.[2] After a time, temple priests who were carrying out repairs discovered an engraved chest at the site of the wall on which Bodhidharma had gazed. In the chest were two texts: the Marrow Cleansing Sutra and the Muscle Modifying Sutra. Marrow cleansing means the cleansing of the mind so that its true light may shine. As for muscle modifying, muscle refers to strength while modifying means to change. As such, muscle modifying means the training of the body to achieve exceptionally strong sinews and bones.

In karate, there are the two styles of Shorin-ryu (少林流) and Shorei-ryu (昭霊流). Shorin-ryu is an abbreviation of Shorinji-ryu (少林寺流)[3] while Shorei-ryu was likely the name given based on the meaning "unity of soul and body" (霊肉一致).

Each of these two styles has its own distinctive character. Shorei-ryu, which reverentially adopted the text of the Muscle Modifying Sutra, strives to achieve a strong body and supple mind chiefly through physical training, while Shorin-ryu places emphasis on the spirit, and therefore seeks to achieve a supple body and strong mind.

In teaching his disciples, Bodhidharma found them spiritually lacking due to inferior physical strength, and lamented how little he was achieving in trying to explain to them the path to enlightenment.

It was then that Bodhidharma realized that teaching

the path to enlightenment necessitated training to cultivate physical and mental fortitude. As a result, he created the Marrow Cleansing and Muscle Modifying Sutras and, in doing so, gave birth to the way of karate. However, as several of Bodhidharma's top disciples who esteemed Shorei Kempo[4] returned to India to pursue what they believed to be the true path of kempo, the monks of the Shaolin Temple focused their energies largely on cleansing the marrow.

I was frequently told these things by Master Azato[5] and I, too, believe that karate originated with Bodhidharma, whose spirit and fists were one.

When master artist Kosugi[6] paid a visit to the Shaolin Temple, he was said to have heard the temple monks speaking of internal achievement and external achievement, which calls to mind a connection with Master Azato's theory regarding supple bodies and strong minds, and also coincides with the scholar Rohan Koda's[7] views. Koda states:

Kempo represents the essence of Shaolin, and while

the Shaolin Temple is where the Zen sect originally took root, it later became the location from which kempo would spread. Later, in novels and assorted books following the Ming Dynasty,[8] a great number of writers expounded on the mysterious wonders of Shorin Kempo. One example cites the ability to kill a man with the flick of a finger. Another speaks of the power of a closed fist to immediately fell any opponent. Xie Zaihang[9] also writes that Shaolin Kempo is unlike anything else in the world and that those who have visited the temple's monks have found each to be the equal of several dozen men.

II

Karate was introduced to Ryūkyū[10] in the fourteenth year of the Keichō era[11] [1609], imported as a natural necessity when weapons were confiscated throughout the land following the invasion of Ryūkyū by Satsuma.[12]

Records indicate that a Chinese man named Kōsōkun[13] brought with him many of his pupils and spread [kempo], and that somebody from the royal castle had gone to study from him. Whatever the case may be, according to these writings, only around 200 years[14] have passed since Kōsōkun's arrival.

According to my thinking, however, I believe that [kempo] arrived a much longer time ago. Because, according to Chinese records, relations between Ryūkyū and China had begun 1,100 years earlier, it is implausible that among the Ryūkyūans who went to China, where kempo flourished, not one of them took lessons, imitating the movements they saw. Rather, it was over the past 200 years that kempo has become popular and many masters have emerged.

Up until the time of my youth, although there were people all around who had trained in China, it seemed that because most of them had placed emphasis on the building of physical strength, they were thought to be considerably inferior in ability to the masters who had trained in Ryūkyū.

Looking at the two styles of Shorei and Shorin from a combat perspective, because Shorei-ryu thrives on mental activity and employs fine technical skills and agility, when fighting at a distance it can beat any opponent, no matter how strong he may be. Since Shorin-ryu places emphasis on strength, it offers an advantage when seizing an opponent and is exceptionally powerful against novices and others with no martial arts knowledge.

Therefore, the study of karate should, by all means, combine some degree of both these two attributes. Through unwavering and persistent training, when the time comes, the appearance of supernatural spiritual powers is the same as with other forms of martial arts.

Although I will not discuss it here, at any rate, it has only been in recent times in Ryūkyū that karate's two styles have blossomed dazzlingly, displaying characteristics that are in complete harmony with one another.

Fundamentally speaking, as the Ryūkyūan race can be viewed as possessing a heredity marked by martial spirit and valor, when weapons became forbidden, the people satisfied their irresistible militaristic urges through such means as tug-of-war and sumo [wrestling] and, in particular, the karate of the castle city of Shuri[15] and surrounding Naha was the focus of admiration among the men of the region.

In the same way that swordsmanship flourished in Japan after Tokugawa[16] brought peace to a country of warring states, karate flourished in Ryūkyū, producing many masters of the art.

III

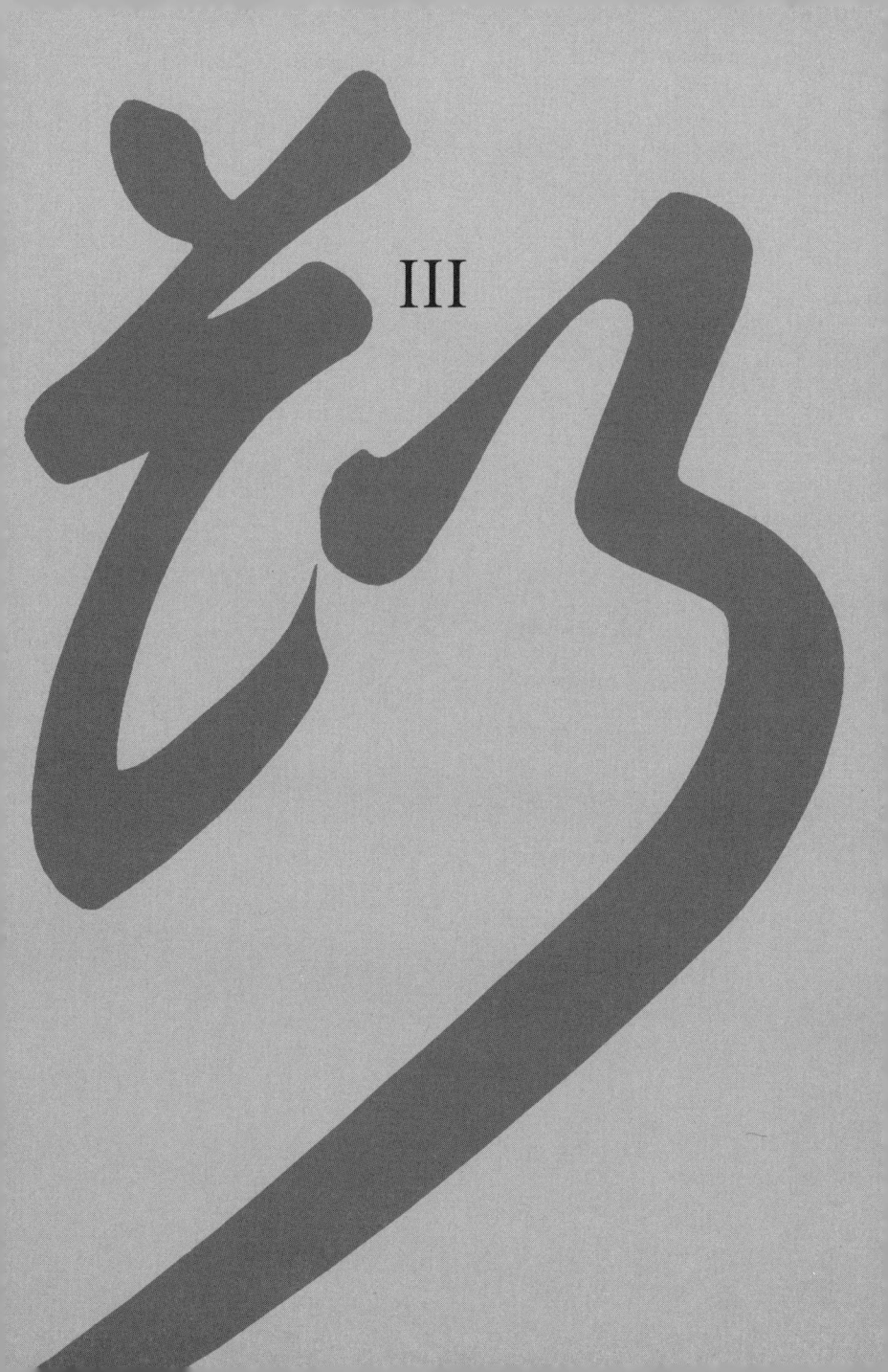

In karate, there are aspects of training that closely resemble acrobatics and there have emerged many masters with various specialties.

Everyone still recalls Makabe the Birdman, the jumping master, who painted the toes of both his feet with ink and, amid a crowd of observers, leapt up from a seated position and delivered a kick, the mark of which remains to this day on the ceiling more than eight *shaku* [approximately 2.4 meters, or 8 feet] above the floor. In short, he was able to escape from any type of difficulty that he might encounter.

And then there was the samurai from Shuri by the name of Tada who, at the age of seventeen, was able to carry four bales containing four *to* [around 72 liters, or 19 gallons] of rice while wearing *geta*[17] and, from around the time he turned twenty, was able to sidestep along a stone wall with the speed of a motorcycle and leap up to a high place even more than one *jō* [approximately 3 meters, or nearly 10 feet] off the ground.

There was also the horse-riding master Hokama who, amid the storm winds of Ryūkyū measuring up to fifty meters per second [180 kilometers, or almost 112 miles, per hour], would stand on a rooftop holding a door against the wind to study strength and balance. Eventually, he was able to support the door in the face of any windstorm.

As for my instructors, the venerable Master Itosu[18] was renowned for his gripping strength and could crush with his hands a Chinese bamboo of four to five *sun* [12–15 centimeters, or 4.75–6 inches] in diameter. Master Azato was expert in the use of spear-hand strikes and had fingertips of incomparable strength. In his youth, he was said to have inadvertently launched a spear-hand strike at a pig in a slaughterhouse and found more than half his hand had penetrated the flesh.

As a boy, I read a storybook about Miyamoto Musashi's encounter with Sekiguchi Yataro at Hakoneyama, during which Miyamoto was certain that he had swept Sekiguchi's legs out from under him only to realize that he had swept through nothing but air. Sekiguchi had apparently vanished without a trace. As Miyamoto stood in disbelief, he soon heard [his opponent's] voice from atop the [shrine's] entryway arch. Although we can assume this to be an exaggerated interpretation of the encounter, to the untrained eye, expertise can yield unimaginable illusions, even those of a person disappearing into thin air.

While those with a strong enough grip to crush a teacup or bamboo ash container with their hands would be capable of [clutching] a thirty *kin* [18 kilograms, or almost 40 pounds] ceramic vat [by its mouth] and carrying it fifteen paces back and forth, in the case of warriors, each has his own inherent nature, which yields its own strong points. As such, it would not be essential for them to display these types of special skills.

The same holds true for breaking roof tiles and boards. Like the practice of test-cutting [of bamboo, rolls of straw, etc.] in Japanese swordsmanship, these could be rightly called avocations. In them, one will not find the true meaning of martial arts. The following story provides a good example.

One of the most highly regarded karate masters in recent Ryūkyū history was Master Matsumura,[19] who in his later years at the royal villa taught many students from Shuri and Naha. One day, on the lawn of the villa, several highly skilled students offered to show the master an unusual demonstration. Curious to see what they would do, Matsumura watched as one of the men broke into a run. The next man immediately gave chase, leapt onto the shoulders of the first, and stood upright. The third member of the group then began chasing after the first two and, in the same fashion, leapt on them and, after climbing up onto the shoulders of the second man, stood upright. This continued until there were five men, one atop the other, loping around the lawn. While the students expected their master to be duly impressed by the performance, Matsumura gave little thought to what he had seen, offering no praise and displaying no astonishment.

In other words, such acrobatic demonstrations, in every regard, represent nothing more than an avocation and have nothing to do with the real path of martial arts. One could even say that they are nothing to fear. As an aside to this story, Master Matsumura's wife also witnessed the students' demonstration and discerned that, among the members, there was one who possessed a disagreeable nature, about which she later warned her husband. That she was able to do so was because, after all, she was a renowned warrior in her own right.

It was karate that brought together Master Matsumura and his wife in marriage, and to this day the story continues to be told. I will add it to this introduction.

Master Matsumura's wife, whose name was Tsurujo, hailed from the Itomine family. At the age of sixteen or seventeen her beauty was well known throughout Shuri and as far away as Naha. One evening, while walking on the outskirts of town, she was attacked by a thug and, after a struggle, managed to narrowly escape harm. Shaken by the incident, she appealed to her father and mother and began diligently training with a then-renowned warrior. The speed with which she gained expertise surpassed that of any man and, by the time Tsurujo turned twenty years old, her master had instilled in her such confidence that he told her the only young man in the entire land that stood a chance of defeating her was probably the son of Matsumura. Following the boost in spirit that she acquired, Tsurujo, like the other young men training in the martial arts, sought to test her courage as well as her skills.

For the skilled martial artists of the time, Naha's red-light district was the place to engage in earnest battle. When evening came, the young people of Shuri would travel nightly to Naha seeking both valor and romance.

Since the city of Shuri is situated on an elevated plateau, upon passing the city's limits the path to Naha leads downhill, with no houses in the vicinity. It was on this path that Tsurujo would lie in wait for young martial artists in training who were headed for Naha, and proceed to hurl every worthy opponent through the air.

Before long, word of Tsurujo's exploits spread and, while the cowardly feared her and kept their distance, those confident in their skills sought her out. But, true to the reputation she had earned, everyone she faced was given a drubbing; no one could defeat her. A young Master Matsumura heard about Tsurujo from friends and pupils and, believing it impossible that a woman could possess such strength, decided to seek out her abilities firsthand.

True to the rumors he had heard, Matsumura soon found himself on the verge of being thrown through the air when he narrowly managed to put an end to the encounter. That was when Tsurujo suddenly grasped Master Matsumura's hand firmly and cheerfully said, "You are the gentleman who will be my husband." Under the circumstances, even the master found himself temporarily bewildered, but ended up surrendering to the young woman's spirited heart and stunning beauty.

I heard about Tsurujo's martial arts skills from Master Matsumura's eldest grandson, who is still alive and is the same age as I. He shared with me the following story.

"At the time, our home was in the brewing business, and whatever rice we were not able to store in the warehouse, we would keep out on the veranda," he said. "When my grandmother would clean the house, I often saw her casually lift a five-*to* [around 90 liters, or 24 gallons] bale of rice with her left hand as she swept the floor underneath with a broom she held in her right hand." Judging by this account, it seems as though she had trained diligently and continued to do so.

IV

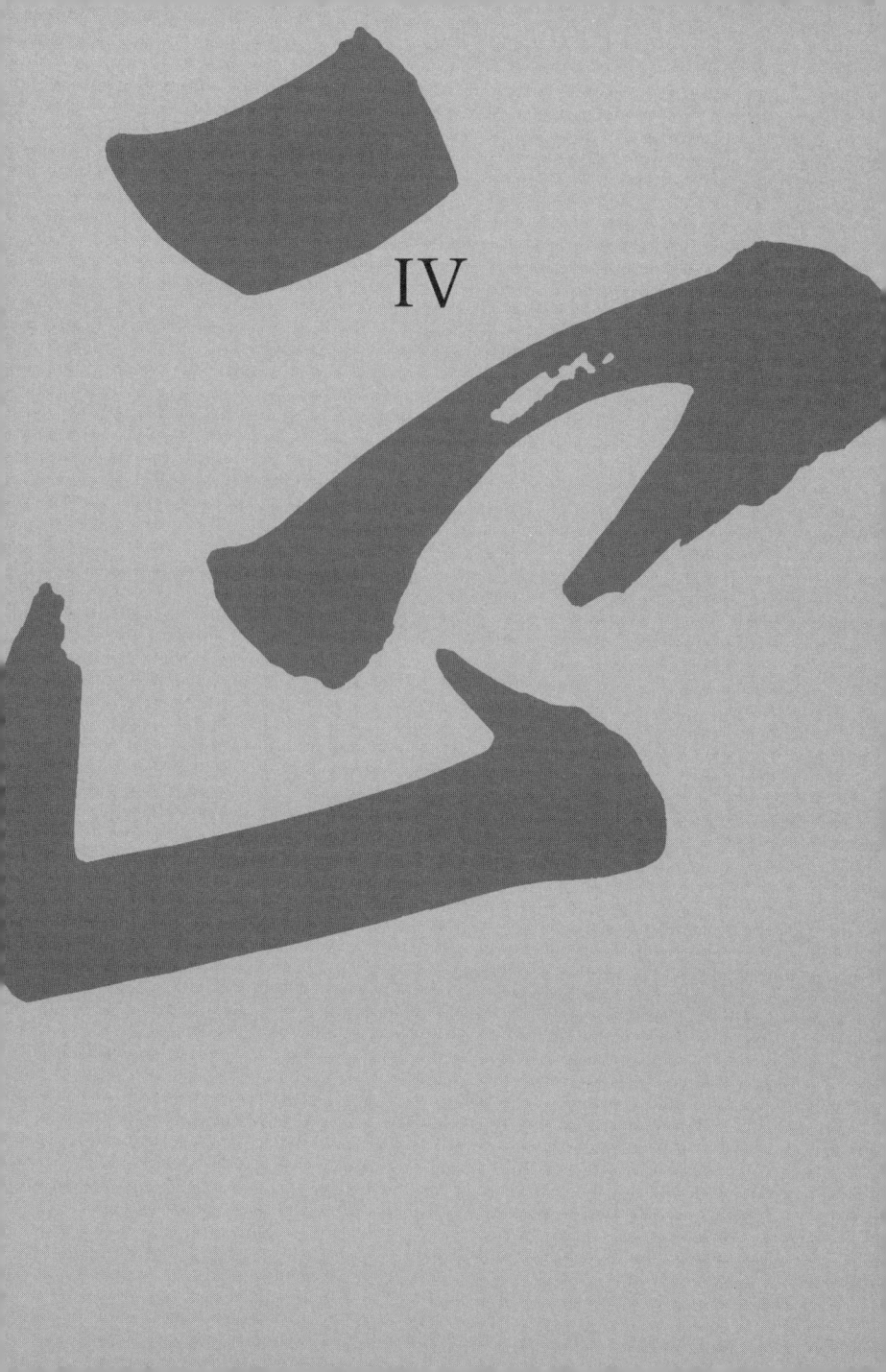

Masters Azato and Itosu, the two teachers from whom I received instruction, were both top disciples of Master Matsumura. As fellow pupils they enjoyed each other's lifelong mutual cooperation and were highly respected within the community.

I came to receive instruction from these two teachers because, before I knew it, I had become acquainted with Master Azato's son, who was three years older than me, and found myself regularly visiting their home.

Master Azato often said that, rather than teach one's own children, it is better to entrust them to someone well qualified, which is why he requested that Master Itosu teach not only his own son but me as well. Since we went to school during the day, we would visit Master Itosu's home for instruction at night. Our training would usually begin in the middle of the night, when people were falling asleep, and continue through dawn, ending as the night gave way to the light of a new day.

Although both Masters Itosu and Azato were brothers in the art of karate, they shared an interesting contrast.

Master Itosu would say that meaningless fights should be avoided, that if someone hits you but causes no harm, then the incident should be taken in stride and forgiven. In contrast, Master Azato, believing that there were no second chances after being dealt a beating, would say that if you provide someone with an opening to strike, you should assume the worst. Master Itosu's words convey tolerance and confidence in a body forged through training while Master Azato's advocate persistent vigilance.

The talents that these two men possessed, in actuality, made obvious this difference in attitudes. One day the two teachers found themselves in a desperate predicament, surrounded by a mob of youths, and were left with no choice but to break free of the throng and beat a retreat. Inquiries afterward revealed that, in the wake of Master Itosu's escape, five or six young men lay unconscious, having received severe thrashings. Along the path that Master Azato had taken, however, were found an exceptionally large number of young men moaning on the ground, albeit they had suffered light beatings.

In terms of social standing, Master Azato was a minor feudal lord in Ryūkyū and, as its last minister of state, he enjoyed direct friendly relations with such notable figures as Prince Itō.[20] He wrote poetry under the pseudonym Rinkakusai and was well versed in Japanese and Chinese studies.

Master Azato received instruction in horsemanship from the Meiji emperor's equerry, Instructor Masachika Megata; in the use of wooden swords from Instructor Yashichiro Ijuin of the Jigen-ryu school of swordsmanship; and in archery from Instructor Genta Sekiguchi. Never tiring of his studies, he would incorporate into his karate the various merits of these sibling martial arts. I was in constant admiration of Master Azato, as he seemed to exemplify the saying "He who truly masters one art possesses versatility in all arts," and had many anecdotes that bore this out.

There was once a man known as "Kanna with the Two-Story Shoulders" who was recognized in Ryūkyū as the top master of the wooden sword.

As one might expect, within Ryūkyū, this man pursued Japanese and Chinese studies and trained in the military arts. The moniker by which he was known, derived from his muscular physique with bulging shoulders that brought to mind a two-story building, extolled his martial arts skills.

I heard, however, that the wooden sword skills of this Kanna with the Two-Story Shoulders proved no match against Master Azato's karate. No matter how many times they faced each other in competition, Kanna ended up bellowing in frustration and disappointment. When I asked the master about these encounters, he answered thus:

"It wasn't that Kanna's martial arts skills were especially lacking in any way. When looking at someone from a martial arts perspective, it is necessary to first gain an understanding of the three Chinese characters used in the study of divination: 満 [pronounced *man*],[21] 寸 [*sun*],[22] and 越 [*etsu*].[23] Because Kanna's nature was that of 満, he would look down on others prior to launching his offensive. As such, anyone who responded to him with either 寸 or 越 would be able to achieve certain victory. Whether he was armed with a wooden sword or was using karate, all one had to do was suddenly present him with an opening, upon which he would grow arrogant and, just like a fish lured by bait, would scorn his opponent and strike. That was his shortcoming."

I eagerly posed many questions to the master. He said to me, "While Confucius advises against teaching one's own child, it was only after I became a father that I was able to understand what this means. So I will tell you what I have to say and I would like for you, in turn, to tell my son when the opportunity arises." Thus, time and again, he would impart his lessons to me. From year to year, I realize that the many lessons he shared with me carry immeasurably significant meaning.

V

"The ability to kill a person with a single blow" is a saying that is often seen and heard in praise of karate but, for karate, this is an undesirable expression.

Likewise, "the ability to kill a person with a single stroke" is used to praise swordsmanship, and "the ability to kill a person with a single shot" to praise shooting. And while similar sayings are also used for archery and spearmanship, for any of the martial arts, should the need ever arise to call upon such skills, anything that lacks the power to kill a person could not be called a martial art.

Because a blow from a bare fist rarely results in any external wounds, there is usually no bleeding, but in the case of someone breathing their last after being struck with a sword or collapsing and dying following a blow from a fist, one cannot draw any conclusions about which of these two approaches might be faster or slower in achieving its objective. In fact, while someone could quickly recover from a superficial wound delivered by a sword, there have also been cases in which a person received a [karate] blow and attached little importance to it, yet died as a result a year or two later.

I am also constantly asked about fighting against weapons but, as is evidenced in tales of bravery from past and present, it must always be remembered that a weapon is merely a tool, while the martial arts reign supreme.

The story of the Yoshioka brothers, who were legendary swordsmen, provides us with a clear example.

One of the Yoshioka brothers went on to become a merchant, turning his back on the martial arts. In his old age he encountered on the street one night an assailant who was intent on testing out his sword on a passerby. As the first strike of the sword approached, Yoshioka swiftly dodged out of its path. The attacker, upon delivering a second strike, discovered that his hand had been grasped and he was immediately thrown forward to the ground. A voice from behind, not even the slightest out of breath, said, "I am Yoshioka. What grudge do you have against me?" The assailant prostrated himself before Yoshioka and begged forgiveness.

A martial artist's strengths or weaknesses are not determined by whether or not he has a weapon; what is essential is his skill.

That karate techniques were something deserving of fear was made known across Kansai [the south-western half of Japan] during the summer of the third year of the Showa era[24] [1928] as a result of the Steel Plate Incident, which took place in Osaka. The man involved in the incident was from an area located five or six *ri* [19.6–23.6 kilometers, or 12.2–14.6 miles] from the city of Naha. Although he was a relative novice to karate, the local news pages of almost every newspaper in Osaka carried the report of how difficult it was to subdue the suspect, an undertaking that required some thirty police officers and took three hours.

Recently, I heard that the appellate court of Nagasaki was tackling the difficult issue of whether or not karate should be deemed a lethal weapon. This development speaks of the mighty power that karate yields.

About six or seven years ago I taught karate at a school for girls, and one day I taught the students three or four self-defense techniques. The next day one of the girls approached me and reported that the previous evening she had been grabbed from behind, just as I had had the students practice. Upon responding to the attack as I had instructed, she managed to throw the large man on his back, driving him some two *ken* [a little more than 3.6 meters, or just less than 12 feet] to the rear.

As for another recent incident, a member of the karate training headquarters, someone with first-dan [black-belt] skills, had been returning late at night to her home outside of the city after having attended an assembly at my place. A man, noticing the young woman walking alone in the dark, approached from behind and called out, offering her a good evening and commenting on how late it was to be out walking the streets. Although she said nothing and continued walking, he persisted in the same manner. As she remained quiet, the man then approached, saying, "Hello there, hello there." This time the woman abruptly turned and asked, "What is it?" Squaring off in a defensive ready posture, she approached and said, "What is your business with me?" The man stopped in his tracks and, clearly intimidated by her fighting spirit, grew flustered and fled the scene.

VI

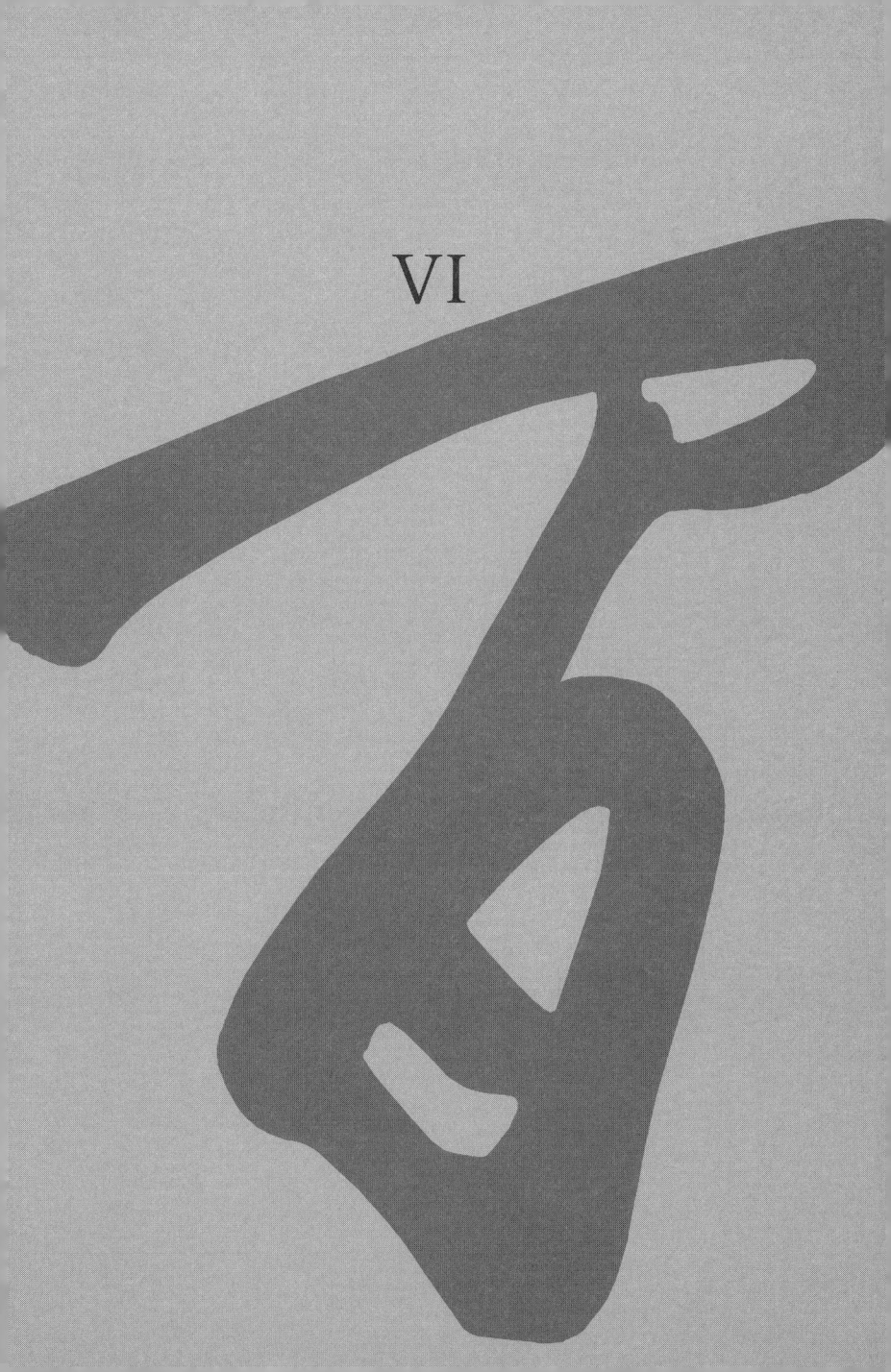

Those who choose to talk about their fights are braggarts who only wish to boast of their victories. When such people lose, it is the other side that does the boasting, which is why they do not feel any particular need to broach the subject. In addition, hotheaded young men who frequently engage in fighting and often find themselves the winners are prone to boast about their strength.

But such things are nothing to brag about.

One day while I was still living in my hometown, I received a visit from a brawny youth who had recently graduated from middle school but was idling away his time at home. The boy boasted to me that he could take on five others in a fight and win. While I assumed that his intention was to show off his prowess, I casually said, "That would be the case if your opponents were weak. Against weak opponents, you could beat ten, even twenty people. But if you were to face someone strong, it is unlikely that you could beat even a single opponent." I then said, "At any rate, show me the best that you can do," and added, "I assure you that I will not strike back."

Although he only managed to lash out recklessly with his fists, the next day he again paid me a visit. I noticed that both of his wrists were wrapped in bandages so, without giving the matter much thought, I asked him if he had been up to no good the night before. He sheepishly said, "No, that is not what happened. The truth is, my wrists became swollen where you had blocked them yesterday."

After that we grew quite close and he became one of my students. And recently an incident that closely resembled this one occurred with another man who also is now a student of mine.

It is safe to say that I have never boasted about striking another person. But I can cite countless examples of winning conflicts without having to resort to fighting. This was the parting lesson left to me by my teachers.

Master Azato often said: "Invincibility in battle does

not make a man virtuous; a virtuous warrior is one who defeats his opponent without engaging in battle." This same thinking also applies to a country's armaments. Because issuing empty threats against an opponent is ineffective, it is only when such threats can be substantiated with ample might that they can be made use of.

The master swordsman Tesshu[25] was in the habit of always cautioning against drawing or using a sword and never once used his sword to take the life of another man. To be fond of battle is, as the proverbs[26] say, like a rice plant that bears no fruit [i.e., lacking in dignity], or the waves that swell in shallow waters [i.e., lacking in intellect]; it is nothing more than the promotion of a discussion completely lacking in any real knowledge.

The following lesson is one that I always make it a point to pass on to young students of karate: In the same way that an adult will indulge an infant's selfish needs, an opponent that you thought to be weak may, in reality, think the same of you and pass you by without acknowledgement.

Herein lies the essence of karate. More important than technique [*jutsu* (術) in Japanese] is the path [*dō* (道)]. That is to say, progressing from the technical aspect of karate to the path that karate itself represents. That is why in Ryūkyū, although the word karate-jutsu does not exist, the word karate-dō is an established term.

There is no first strike in karate—this is what I deem to be the essence of karate-dō.

In other words, respond to your opponent once he moves, without initiating the action. He who is able to read circumstances in his mind before they transpire, to see the playing out of opposing forces yet to begin, as if with eyes behind one's head, is capable of knowing the path to certain victory.

The blade of a sword that only slices through the air may be duller than lead, but a poised and ready iron fist contains power great enough to kill. He who initiates the action invites his own opportunity for death. When hunting an eagle, only the scoundrel shoots before it has taken wing. The man who acts first, even if he presents himself as a sage, behaves in the manner of one who is ignorant of human folly, is incapable of seeing with the eyes of the heart. Only those who follow the proper path at all times are able to gain a command of movement that transcends established methods, and grasp a true understanding of techniques.

Karate has more than twenty kata.[27] Like textbooks to a student or tactical exercises to a soldier, kata are the most important element of karate. Regardless of the kata, each represents fairness for all to see, a sense of humility towards others, adherence to reason, and the proper use of martial arts.

In the past, masters would first look at the character of potential students before agreeing to teach them. Those whose natures were deemed inappropriate, even in the case of one's own child, were strictly forbidden from receiving training in the martial arts. Conversely, through karate, it was possible to pacify those with a violent temperament.

Teachers at the schools where I teach speak to me at great length about their students who train in karate, telling me about how they have become more restrained in their behavior. For me, such stories are a source of pride and satisfaction.

VII

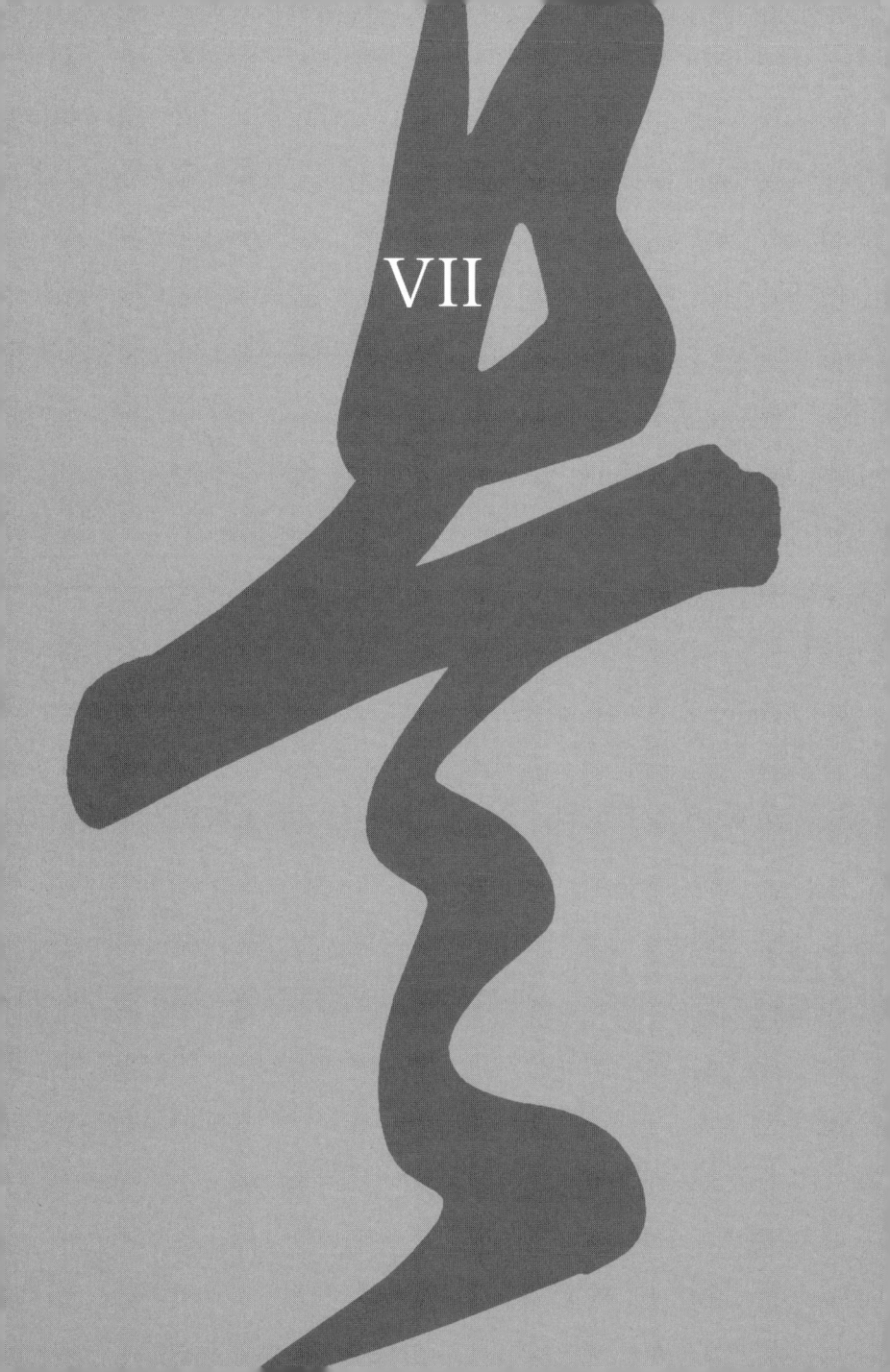

In the summer of the eleventh year of the Taisho era[28] [1922], I traveled to Tokyo with three scrolls[29] to take part in the Ministry of Education's First Annual Athletic Exhibition as a representative of karate.

Following the event, I conveyed a message to Master Kano[30] offering to visit his private residence to give him a demonstration of karate. He gladly welcomed me but said that he would prefer a larger audience than just himself, so I told him that I would return in two days to provide a demonstration and explanation.

Many high-ranking judo practitioners attended the demonstration and Master Kano had invited more than eighty students from Tomisaka-shita[31] to watch. The master actively made a hands-on study of the presentation and, after posing a variety of queries, asked the high-ranking judo practitioners whether they had any questions to ask. It was at that time that the current ninth-dan black belt Yamashita[32] inquired about the arm that I had left extended following the demonstration of a punching technique. He asked why I had not retracted my fist following the punch. While this might seem a trivial matter, the question revealed considerable insight and I responded without hesitation that a subsequent technique can be launched immediately after punching.

A related story that I am reminded of was the time I demonstrated karate to Instructor Yagyu[33] and the late General Yashiro at the Hekikyō-Kan training hall of the eleventh-generation Yagyu Tajima no Kami,[34] located in Ushigome Wakamatsu-chō [Tokyo].

I brought along with me an experienced karate student from my hometown to take part in the demonstration, during which the student attacked with a kick. I blocked his leg with my arm and immediately found my fist hurling toward his face, using the exchange to explain the need to free the mind.

Instructor Yagyu, appearing to immediately understand the significance of my demonstration, said, "Although

[our] family tradition states that no limits should be placed on technique, all martial arts share the same spirit!"

Master Azato constantly spoke of and advocated an understanding of the laws of yin and yang [negative and positive cosmic forces], invoking the old saying: Battle lies between *ki* (気)[35] and *sei* (正);[36] without converting ki into sei, and sei into ki, there would be no way to achieve victory. It is a given that karate, as well, adheres to the fundamental principle of martial arts in that attacks quickly become blocks and blocks are transformed into attacks.

VIII

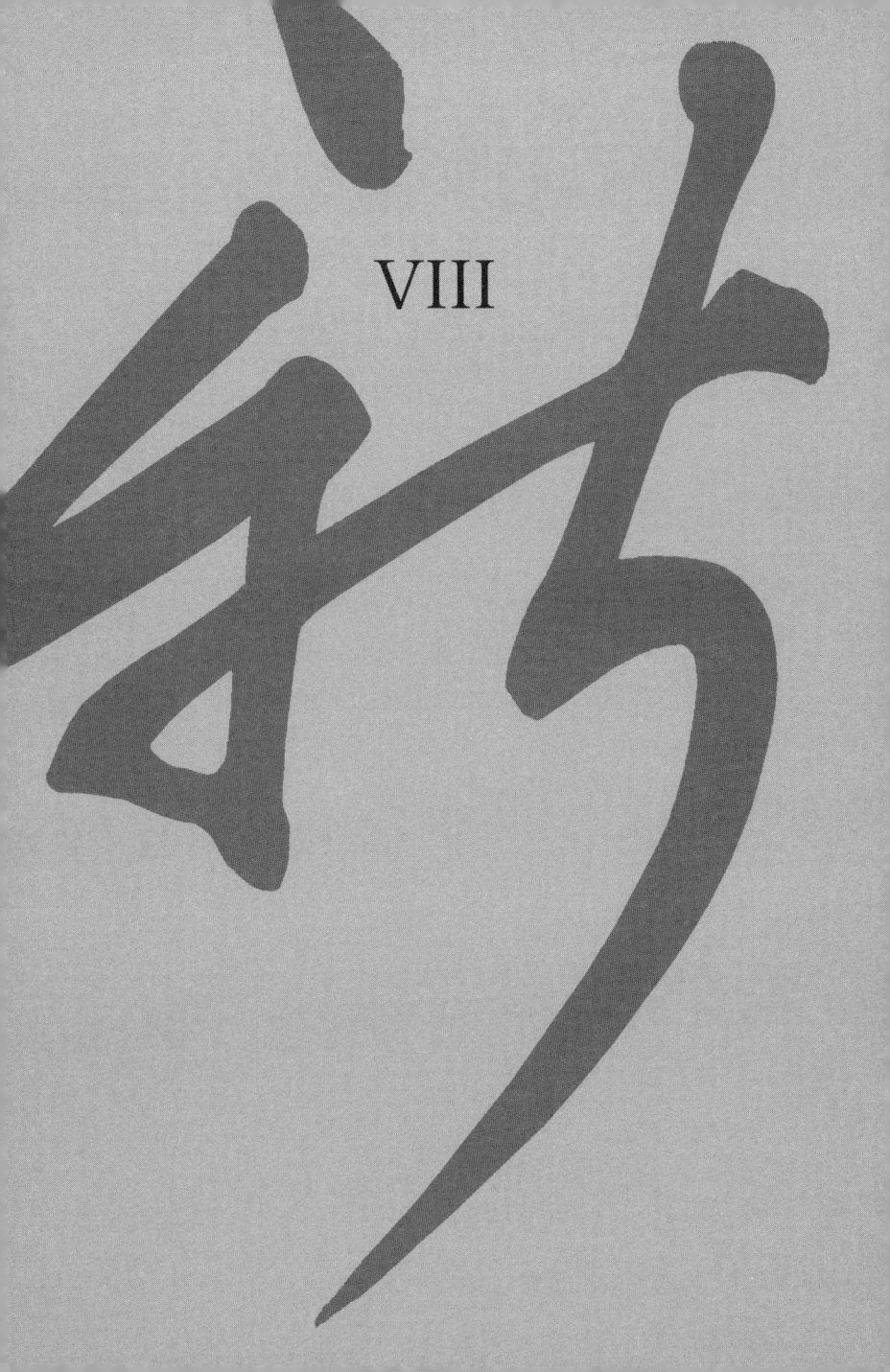

Today there are no young people in such areas as Tokyo and Osaka who are not familiar with the word karate, an indication of just how widespread the art has become. The number of people training in karate has grown considerably, and I now offer instruction at nine different high schools and universities. Each passing day sees karate increase in popularity, with some people training individually while others participate in group lessons held at the boarding houses of department stores or other locations.

When I first came to Tokyo, however, it was karate's age of unenlightenment, so to speak; I never dreamed at the time that karate would enjoy the level of popularity it does today.

Making use of all the contacts available to me, I gave demonstrations here and there and intended to return home as scheduled. It was just at that time when I received a request to teach a karate course from the Poplar Club, a social club centered around master artist Misei Kosugi. Of course I was delighted to accept the invitation. At the club, I recall meeting such members as the Tennis Association's Mr. Harishige[37] and the great artist Tsuruzo Ishii.[38]

Speaking of the artist Kosugi, because he had once visited my hometown, I was familiar with his name but only learned upon our first meeting that, in private, he was an avid exercise enthusiast.

From that time on, he trained in karate continuously for more than ten years and, whenever there was a karate-related gathering at which he made a speech or said a few words, he would take the opportunity to pay me a compliment, saying he was Master Funakoshi's first student in Tokyo.

The weeklong karate course at the Poplar Club was very enjoyable and on the evening of the final day a dinner banquet was held in my honor. It was at that banquet that the distinguished artist said that, since I would be returning to my hometown, there would be no one for him to go to should he have a question to ask concerning karate. As such, he said that he would like for me to prepare something in writing about the subject.

Even though I had drunk quite a bit, upon returning that night to the prefectural student dormitory where I was staying, I promptly began working on the framework for what I would write. By the following morning I had prepared the outline for an entire book and, over the next several days, finished writing all of the text. The book, entitled *Karate Jutsu*, is now in its tenth printing. After completing the manuscript, I wasted no time in paying Mr. Kosugi a visit to show him my work. When I saw him, he commented on the great speed with which I had responded to his request, revealing to me just how surprised and impressed he was with my effort. But, the artist informed me, when he had asked me to write about karate, he had meant an article to appear in a magazine. I, however, had jumped to my own conclusion and written an entire book.

Whenever the artist gets the opportunity, he enjoys joking about the episode. He will say that I take a karate-like approach to writing books: in other words, I do so with great speed.

A person's destiny is indeed a peculiar thing—it was Mr. Kosugi's brief request for me to write about karate and my misunderstanding of what he had meant that led to my staying in Tokyo for more than ten years rather than returning to my hometown two or three days hence.

If the artist had not said what he did at the time, or if I had not misunderstood him and had only written a short magazine article that night, I am certain that I would have returned to my hometown two or three days later as originally planned. Even if I were to have again traveled to Tokyo, it most likely would have been after spending four or five years in my hometown. Consequently, it would seem that, at times, a misunderstanding can have very favorable outcomes.

I wasn't thinking of spending a lengthy amount of time in Tokyo, but what first stopped me as I was readying to return to my hometown was the karate course I held at the Poplar Club.

IX

I am now sixty-six years old. I began learning karate at the age of twelve or thirteen and, since that time, not a single day has passed that I have not trained.

Such a claim, however, is not unique to just me, as it also applies to almost anyone who studies karate.

So, I have been practicing karate now for some fifty-four or -five years. But, when considering my current age compared to the longevity of my instructors and other recent martial arts masters, I realize that I still have a long way to go.

To offer some examples, I shall mention the ages of the predecessors with whom I have had a direct relationship. Master Azato passed away at the age of eighty, while Master Itosu lived to the age of eighty-five and, up to that time, commuted every day by horse to a teachers college where he taught the students. And Master Matsumura, who trained both Masters Azato and Itosu, lived even longer, passing away at ninety-three.

Although you may assume that these men were physically fit by nature, the opposite was the case for all of them, as Master Azato and others were quite sickly in their boyhood. It was due to their weak constitutions that they began practicing karate.

In fact, as a child, I suffered from a very weak stomach until I started training in karate. Every day I would carry my bottle to receive medicine at the home of the doctor whose family had, for seven generations, served as attending physicians to the king of Ryūkyū.

Once I started karate, however, it would seem that my ailment was afraid of karate, as it disappeared, and I have not succumbed to illness for even a single day since that time. While this may sound somewhat far fetched, it happens to be entirely true. For twenty-three years I supported primary school education and, it goes without saying, I missed not a single day of work.

There was an incident that happened not long ago. I was returning home from a university by train at midday.

The train was fairly empty, but there was one drunken man who was making quite a bit of noise. After looking around this way and that, he cast his gaze on my face and promptly headed in my direction. As I was wondering what he intended to do, he drew his face to mine and began sniff-sniffing away at the air around my mouth and nose.

The man exercised his sense of smell for a while before speaking. He said, "You've not had anything to drink, right?" When I told him that he was correct, the drunken man drew back and, after gazing intently at my face, assumed an entirely different tone of voice. Offering me praise on my face, he said, "I must say, sir, that your face has a vibrant color to it. In fact, your complexion is quite splendid!" The other passengers on the train had been directing their attention to us and clearly enjoyed a good laugh at this spectacle.

Incidentally, I would like to add one more story on the topic of color.

While I was living in my hometown, a wealthy

gentleman who always enjoyed the finest of meals, taking notice of my complexion, said, "It is clear that you follow a very nutritious diet; I would like for you to share with me some of your secrets." While I responded truthfully, informing him that I followed a very simple diet and had never given any special thought to eating nutritious meals, he found it difficult to accept my response.

With regard to this subject, I maintain a belief about a person's complexion.

This is, of course, something that everyone knows. Although quite simple and in no way philosophical, in short, by exercising each part of the body in moderation, all of the body's functions will become robust on their own, leading to healthy circulation and an improved complexion. I once heard from a doctor that people with a weak stomach suffer from blood congestion, as one-third of the body's blood becomes concentrated in that area. It is only natural that such people would appear pale; it would be necessary to call it a wonder if they were to have vibrant coloring.

Along with the matter of complexion, I would also like to comment on the body. There was an incident that occurred six or seven years ago, around the time that I reached the age of sixty, while I was teaching karate to students of Tokyo Imperial University.[39]

My third son[40] was also working there and, as I returned home one day, he told me that earlier in the day one of the university's teachers had seen me leading a class of students and had commented to him, "Your father is quite young. He looks only about forty years old."

Even now, people from my hometown who I have known since long ago continue to mention my youthful appearance, telling me that there is an imbalance between my age and my body. And this is not mere flattery as, based on assessments by the general public, it seems as though there is a discrepancy between my age and my physical appearance.

Personally, however, my thinking contradicts the opinions of others, as I would like for my body to be even more youthful; I would have no objections to such being the case. Just because the years accumulate and we grow older, I do not believe that there is such a need for the body to rush toward feebleness as it advances ever closer to the grave.

X

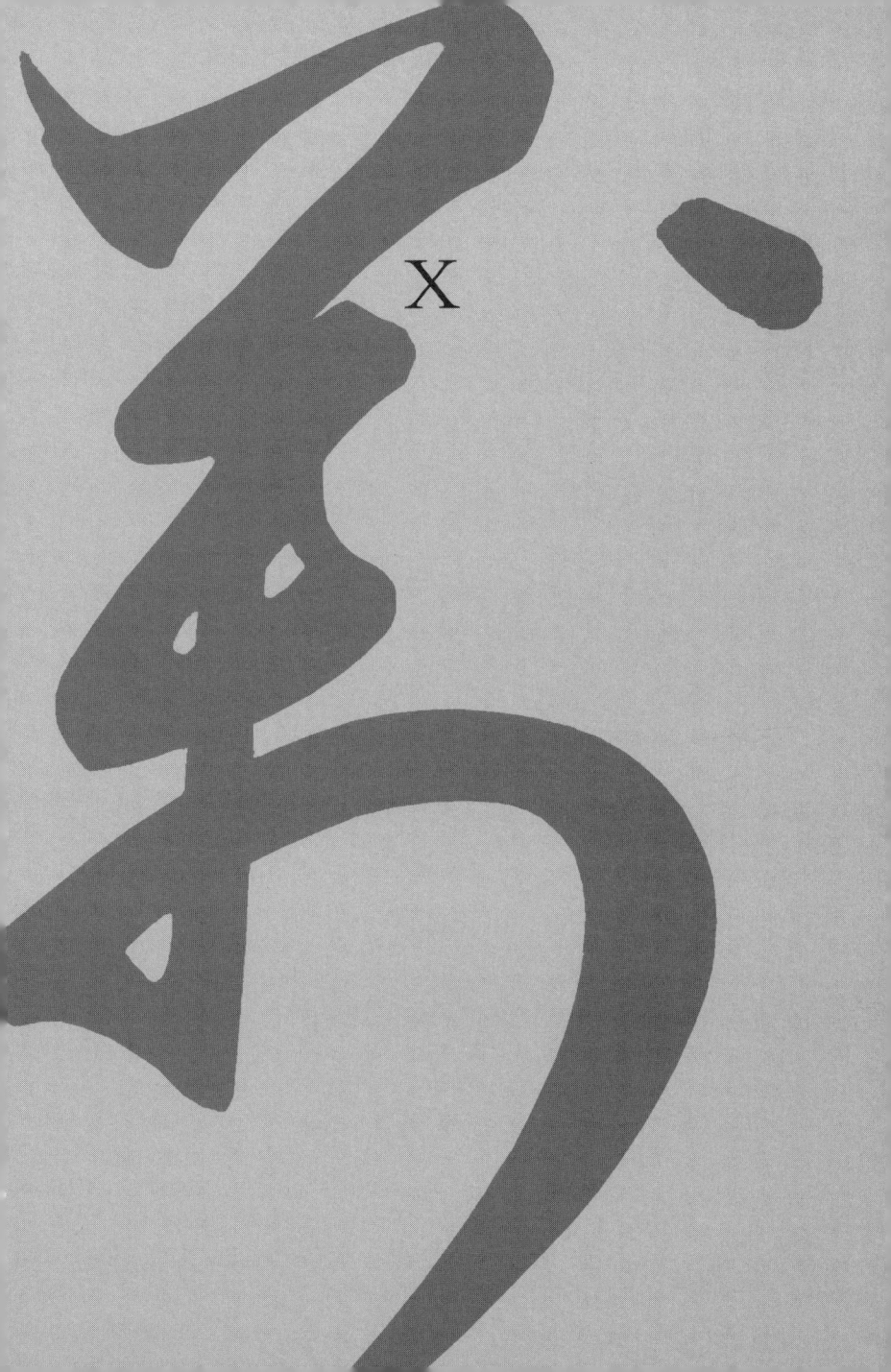

I believe the question of mind and body to be an essential issue.

While I was living in my hometown, almost every year I was asked to serve as a referee for the Naminoue Shrine prefectural sumo tournament. In connection with this responsibility, I had checked the ages of all the competing athletes from each prefecture. Although one accepted theory states that the average age at which human physical strength peaks is twenty-five, according to my inquiry, I discovered it to be twenty-six.

There was one man, however, who proved to be an exception. He lived just four *ri* [15.7 kilometers, or 9.8 miles] from the city of Naha, where the prefectural office is located, and was a well-known sumo wrestler throughout the prefecture. Even at the age of forty, he competed as a representative of his county. Because I sensed something special in his resolve, I ranked him in the upper division, determined to have him either retire should he lose, or bask in success should he win. Of course, his opponent was a strong man recognized as the prefecture's top competitor.

The sumo of Okinawa differs from the conventional form of the sport, as the contestants begin from a locked position, and even if their hands or knees should touch the ground it does not result in a loss. Rather, a contestant loses only when he is thrown on his back. Matches are decided in three rounds and, as the contestants grapple with one another, it is rare that someone loses a match due to injury.

Returning to the story of the forty-year-old wrestler, however, he claimed victory in grand style, repeatedly hurling his large, younger opponent through the air.

I have heard that, according to scholars and doctors, the human body is in its prime between the ages of fifteen and forty, but upon reaching thirty, most people tend to withdraw from athletic competition. At that age, however, not only has the body not declined in the least, but there is also still room for improvement. As such, withdrawing from competition is the same as conceding defeat.

Forty-five years ago, the winner of the Tokyo–Osaka All-Japan Marathon was a forty-year-old man from Hokkaido. Also, the first champion of the sumo tournament sponsored by the *Nichi-Nichi Shimbun* [newspaper] was the former [professional sumo wrestler] Tochigiyama, who had reached the age of forty after having retired [from professional sumo]. There is also a man more than sixty years old who practices running for marathons daily, and his performance is no different from those of younger men. While it depends on the nature of the athletic competition, according to my thinking, I feel that by firmly maintaining an indomitable spirit and believing in the body's abilities, with diligent continued training, there is absolutely no reason for a person to become immobile, even at the age of sixty, or seventy.

In Okinawa, elderly men are called *tanmei* [literally, "short-life"].[41] Although this is an impolite way in which to refer to those of advanced age, elderly people who practice karate are called *bushi tanmei* ["warrior short-life"][42] and are duly feared, as their strength increases with age. It should be noted that, in this case, "bushi" refers to a martial artist and not a member of the warrior class.

Such thinking is not based on simple preconceptions. Recent masters of Ryūkyū karate, provided that they were not deathly ill, wielded immeasurable amounts of strength.[43] Their expert students forty or fifty years of age, as well as young students with great physical strength, regardless of how hard they may have tried, were no match against these masters.

There is nothing surprising about this. All one has to do is think about Japan's martial arts masters of the past, or the various current masters, who have become increasingly stronger as they have grown older.

Additionally, in Okinawa, bushi tanmei are known as *koijin*.[44] Boiled down to its most basic meaning, "koijin," as it turns out, is a person with a healthy sexual appetite. On top of having a robust body through training and maintaining the will to grow stronger step by step during one's lifetime, by feeling young, it is only natural that these men should be nothing like those elderly people who have grown feeble in old age. There are many businessmen, politicians, and others as well who increase their vigor as they grow older, not as a result of physical training, but because they are vivacious, maintaining a feeling of youth.

The other day, I accompanied some young people to Shiobara [in Tochigi Prefecture, north of Tokyo], wearing my usual low wooden fair-weather *geta* as we strolled around the mountainside. One of the people in the group, looking askance at my footwear, said, "How are you able to walk around the mountains in those geta without falling down?" In Tokyo, there are two or three universities that have moved to the suburbs where I dash around daily wearing low wooden geta, but I have yet to ever fall or find myself short of breath. I am confident that, throughout my life, I will not lose my physical freedom of movement.

In short, because karate came about to prevent the decline of the spirit and atrophying of physical strength, what would have been the benefit of the more than fifty years that I have dedicated to training should I find myself falling down? While it is easy to fall prey to delusions in our youth, as we get older we are not so easily deceived. As such, because we are better able to see the movement of an opponent's hands and our bodies feel lighter and move with greater freedom, we are able to polish our techniques.

XI

In closing, I would like to briefly highlight the characteristics of karate.

It is safe to say that karate begins and ends with kata. In kata, when one begins from the right, the same movement will be repeated to the left; upon moving forward, the same distance is traveled in return. If the right hand is used, then the left hand will be used in the same way; when the right leg kicks, then the left leg also will kick in the same way. In this way, the entire body is made use of without favoring any one part over another, enabling all the parts of the body to move in harmony and unity without special effort, and because each individual movement has meaning against an imagined opponent, it makes things all the more interesting.

On top of this, karate can be practiced by oneself, anytime and anywhere, without having to rely on others, making use of just two or three minutes of spare time. As each individual is free to make his training either difficult or simple, karate is well suited for everyone, regardless of age, gender, or physical condition.

Karate also offers outstanding benefits when viewed from a physical education perspective, which is why it has been approved by the Ministry of Education as part of the middle school educational curriculum in Okinawa prefecture.

While karate is not something that can be easily conveyed and is difficult to explain without presenting an actual demonstration, a characteristic that distinguishes it as karate is that it cannot be commercialized or adapted for competition. Herein lies the essence of karate-dō, as it cannot be realized with protective equipment or through competitive matches.

It was March of the tenth year of the Taisho era [1921].

His current majesty,[45] who was crown prince at the time, was en route to Europe and brought the imperial carriage to a stop in Okinawa prefecture to pay a visit.

An audience of some six hundred thousand welcomed His Imperial Highness's arrival and, while six varieties of entertainment were proposed to the crown prince's entourage, the only one to be selected was karate. I was entrusted with the responsibility of training the athletes, providing me with the honor of a lifetime. I was later delighted to hear that His Imperial Highness, well acquainted with the literary and military arts, had expressed his appreciation for the karate demonstration.

Indeed, karate was originally developed to condition the mind and body, cultivating vitality toward the creation of competent individuals to benefit the whole of the country while also providing a "life-giving sword"[46] against lawless and foolhardy gangs. The flower of karate that blossomed in Ryūkyū, having spread far and wide throughout our country [Japan], has borne fruit and will, I believe, contribute to launching the Japanese race onto the world stage.

AFTERWORD
Remembering Old-Man Gichin

The members of our family would reverentially call Old-man[1] Gichin [Funakoshi] "Uncle Ufudunchi."

Ufudunchi[2] is an honorific title directed toward the main branch of the family. However, as for that uncle—Old-man Gichin spent a long time in Tokyo and only a few members of the family had the pleasure of meeting him. Even so, in addition, from an early age I had been told, as a matter of pride to the family, that Old-man Gichin was a *bushi* [warrior] and a teacher of karate at universities in Tokyo.

Looking at the Funakoshi family lineage, Old-man Gichin and my father were cousins. My father and uncles had been taught by Old-man Gichin—he was a teacher (trainer) at the Naha Ordinary Elementary School at the time—before he had gone to Tokyo.

The Funakoshi family belongs to the warrior class, and Old-man Gichin's childhood name was Umigamī.[3] When a child is born in a warrior-class family, he is given a childhood name. In addition, there is a "given name initial character." Within the Funakoshi family, this character is 義.[4] Aside from this proper given name there is a Chinese name. The Funakoshi family's is Yō.[5] Because Old-man Gichin was born in the Ryūkyū Kingdom era, he surely had a Chinese name, which was probably something like Yō Gijin.[6]

Because Old-man Gichin was a warrior, the Funakoshi name was frequently thought to be of military lineage, but aside from Old-man Gichin there were no warriors in the family. Rather, [the family's background is concentrated in] the arts. Old-man Gichin had a keen interest in the arts as well. He was quite fond of traditional Okinawan and Chinese poetry. He was familiar with Chinese books and Okinawan history. But more than anything else, in that he persevered in his lifelong conviction of cultivating the literary arts while training in the military arts, I discovered Old-man Gichin to be the ideal educator.

I went to Tokyo during the summer of the fifteenth year of the Shōwa era[7] [1940] and, for a little more than three years, until the winter of the eighteenth year [of the same era], was taken care of by Old-man Gichin's second son Giyu.

It was during that time that I had the opportunity to meet Old-man Gichin.

Around that time Giyu lived in Tenjinchō in Ushigome, while Old-man Gichin lived in Zōshigaya. On Sundays, Uncle Giyu (which is what I called him) would often send me on errands to Zōshigaya.

Old-man Gichin also would show up in Tenjinchō from time to time. Old-man Gichin had three sons living in Tokyo. His eldest son Giei lived in Hayashichō (now Sengoku) in Koishikawa; his second son was Giyu; and the third son Gigo, who was regarded as Old-man Gichin's successor, taught karate at the dojo [training hall] in Zōshigaya.

Every time I would go to Zōshigaya, Gigo would always call out to me: "Hey! Come over to the dojo!"

As I suffered from weak knees, I was frightened of karate. It was Old-man Gichin who saved me from having to go to the dojo.

Old-man Gichin would call me up to his study on the second floor. That is where my eyes were opened to Okinawan history. And that was around the time that I learned the names Sai On,[8] Tei Junsoku,[9] and Heshikiya Chōbin.[10] This was when my interest in the history of my homeland began to grow.

When I think of Old-man Gichin, I only recall him wearing Japanese-style clothes.

And these were elaborate outfits for each of the four seasons, and when he went out, he wore a formal *hakama* [a pleated skirt-like garment worn by men]. Even when at home, I don't recall ever having seen him dressed casually or sitting cross-legged. His manners and behavior were indeed quite proper. It seemed to me as though there was a rhythm to his movement.

However, there was one exception. That was when he would make a dash for a train that was about to depart. This story requires some background explanation.

Old-man Gichin would occasionally pay a visit to his second son Giyu's home, where I was boarding at the time, and it was my job to see him back to the metropolitan streetcar stop when it was time for him to go home. The stop was Yaraishita. The stop was at one end of the streetcar line.

That was when Old-man Gichin would dash off.

Raising the umbrella (this was not a substitute for a cane; it was a parasol) and cloth bag which he always carried with him, he would take off running while crying out, "Wait!" It was a spectacular sight to behold.

Old-man Gichin's footwear was wooden geta.[11] They were tall and heavy. It was widely acknowledged at the time that people in their seventies were advanced in age and, accordingly, considered to be quite old.

There were some people who expressed their concern: "Should you be wearing those geta? Old man, what would happen if you were to suffer a fall?" But what was surprising at the time was that he ran around wearing those tall and heavy wooden geta as if he were a young man.

Watching that as a boy of fifteen, a thought occurred to me: "Uncle is a true warrior."

From the end of December of year sixteen of the Shōwa era [1941] to the start of January the following year, Old-man Gichin returned to Okinawa. Twenty years had passed since he went to Tokyo and it was his first trip home. It would also be his last visit to his hometown.

Uncle Giyu and I accompanied him on the trip. The ship was the *Kaijō Maru*. Upon arriving in port, newspaper reporters poured into the ship's salon. During our stay there were constant receptions. Uncle Giyu was practically pulling his hair out but Old-man Gichin thought nothing of attending the banquets day after day and night after night. As I was still a minor, I was not able to join Old-man Gichin at the banquets, although an exception was made on one occasion. It was the Funakoshi family banquet. It was most likely a farewell party. I recall my father telling me later that I was granted special permission to attend because I had accompanied Old-man Gichin on the trip and would be returning with him. At this banquet I witnessed something wonderful. It was Old-man Gichin's dancing.

In Okinawa there is a dance called the Kachāshī. The person performing it dances freely, from the heart. This dance, which does not follow any particular etiquette, must be danced by those in attendance at the closing of a banquet. There is no getting out of it. Old-man Gichin's turn had come. Slightly drunk, he stood up and, as he started dancing, he tied his headband in the front. This is a trick that only someone quite experienced would be able to pull off. But that was not the only thing. There was a unique quality to Old-man Gichin's Kachāshī that only he could achieve. In Tokyo, I doubt that he ever had the opportunity to dance the Kachāshī. If so, why was he was able to dance it [after such a long time]? While I may get in trouble for saying so, I believe that it was because his movements had been refined through karate training.

I was [also] impressed that, even though Old-man Gichin had been isolated from the Okinawan language, he was able to elegantly speak without hesitation in the Shuri dialect.

From Naha to Kobe, the sea was rough. The Bungo Channel was particularly awful. Neither Uncle Giyu nor I was able to eat.

As for Old-man Gichin, however, when the time came, he would get ready and leave for the dining hall. I was later told that the ship's captain, who sat at the same table, had been astounded.

Old-man Gichin's nom de plume was "Shoto." I once asked him about the origin of the name. I recall it was the seventeenth year of the Shōwa era [1942]. At the time, he told me the following story:

> As a boy I would often go to play at such places as Torazuyama and Ōnoyama. Torazuyama is a hill in Shuri and Ōnoyama is an outer islet upstream from

Naha Port. Both have abundant pine groves and, renowned for their tranquil surroundings, were enjoyed by many as popular destinations for outings.

I also frequently went to these places. I even went alone on occasion.

One day I became aware of the sound of the wind sweeping across the pine grove. The sound of the pine grove resonated exactly like surging waves. When I looked up, the undulations of the pine grove itself were already surging waves. However, they were not fierce, aggressively pounding waves. It was a relaxed swaying. Furthermore, the green color was symbolic of spring. The waves created by the pine grove were powerful and abundant, but also gentle.

It was then that I made up my mind. When I became an adult, I would adopt the pseudonym "Shoto."[12]

Old-man Gichin was educated in the Chinese classics. With regard to learning, the earnest attitude he maintained never diminished.

The ideals he held of "cultivating the literary arts while training in the military arts" and "karate as a martial art for men of virtue" were born as a result. I feel that his creation of a university karate club provides a glimpse of his intentions.

There is an episode I would like to introduce.

I had an uncle by the name of Kamata. He was still young, so this was before Old-man Gichin had left for Tokyo, around the time that he was teaching at an elementary school in Naha. Uncle asked to receive karate lessons, but Old-man Gichin promptly turned him down. He said, "Kamata, you have a violent temperament. You lose control of yourself when you drink. I hear that you are always getting into fights. What would happen if I were to teach you karate?"

Later in his life, that uncle reminisced [about the episode].

He said, "It was a good thing that I never received karate training. If I had acquired martial arts skills, I may have inflicted injury on someone. Uncle Ufudunchi made good decisions: he was a good judge of character."

Even in old age, that uncle had a violent temper and would boast about winning fights.

Since I lived near Old-man Gichin, I regret that there were so many things that I should have asked him about.

In the end, I never asked to hear about [what it was like] before and after the abolition of the feudal domains;[13] about his youth when his father and grandfather, who belonged to the Obstinate Party,[14] had refused to cut off their topknots; or about his grandfather Gifuku, who was responsible for preparing meals for the court of Kikoe-Ōkimi.[15] Although it is true that I was not old enough at the time to take an interest in such topics, how unfortunate it is [that I never asked him about them].

Mr. Fuyū Iha, in his essay *Trends in Ryūkyū History* (*Iha Fuyū Zenshū* [The Collected Works of Fuyū Iha]; Volume 1: *Old Ryūkyū*, p. 59. Heibonsha Ltd. Publishers), states the following:

What Sai On conveyed to King Shō Kei[16] as advice has since been passed on from the time of King Shō Kei to this day. What was said was this:

"[Maintaining peaceful diplomatic relations] with China is not particularly difficult, and even if any difficulty should arise, someone from Kumejima[17] would be able to set things to rights. However, [diplomatic relations] with Japan[18] are another matter. The day will likely come when a letter will arrive and the king will be forced to abdicate his reign, but [that letter] will come not from China, but rather from Japan."

That is what was said. One year, around the time when people air out [their clothes], King Shō Tai[19] explained this to Mr. Azato, who conveyed it to me through Mr. Funakoshi, [who was] instructing at the Naha Ordinary Elementary School. (Excerpt from the original text)

The "Mr. Funakoshi" here refers to a young Old-man Gichin, while "Mr. Azato" refers to Azato Yasutsune,

Old-man Gichin's karate teacher. Azato Yasutsune served as chief attendant to King Sho Tai and was also a martial arts master.

I feel that this story has historical significance as an illustration of Sai On's insight, his incredible ability to see what lay ahead in the future, and I believe that Old-man Gichin had many such stories [that he could have imparted].

As for tales of his own heroic exploits, Old-man Gichin had none.

Old-man Gichin was, however, successful in building character through karate. He paved the way for karate to become a global martial art. He could be called both an outstanding warrior and an educator. Of this I have no doubt.

Shinken Taira,[20] a well-known instructor of kobudo [ancient weapons fighting], was also a student of Old-man Gichin's.

At the time, Mr. Taira had a kobudo and karate dojo in Ikaho[21] and, on occasion, would come to Tokyo to pay a visit to Old-man Gichin at the Shotokan dojo in Zōshigaya. For some reason, instead of going straight to Zōshigaya, this Instructor Taira would make it a habit of first stopping at the Funakoshi residence in Tenjinchō to take me along with him.

It wasn't that he was unfamiliar with the geography of Tokyo. There was no need to provide him with directions. Later, I realized that he simply wanted me to accompany him to carry the souvenirs [he brought], but I recall that Mr. Taira was always formally dressed in Japanese-style attire.

When he paid visits to Old-man Gichin, on most occasions I was permitted to join them [during their conversations].

With regard to young people and the path of karate, they did not discuss matters of battle, but rather spoke about Okinawa, and even then they would mainly reminisce. They would talk about nature, and about the Tsuji red-light district [in Naha]. That was when Old-man Gichin would suddenly turn to me and ask, "Do you know the saying 'For boys, gaining age comes with ease, gaining knowledge with difficulty'?"

When I answered, "Yes, I know it," he said with a smile, "Well, there is another saying that is based on it."

"'Seeking pleasure comes with ease, making money with difficulty. A six-yen monthly salary is not to be looked down upon; although I have still to wake from yesterday's dream of Tsujimachi,[22] all of a sudden I hear word this morning of my dismissal.'"

It was understood around town that a policeman, who, because of his profession, was banned from visiting the red-light district, had made the saying up. I was told that the average monthly salary at the time (probably the Meiji era [1868–1912]) was six yen. And even now I remember it, which shows how strong an impression the story must have made on me.

While such stories may have been too soft for young warriors seated facing one another with their legs folded beneath them, this too was yet another side of Old-man Gichin.

Old-man Gichin would also talk about the history of the Tsuji red-light district, about the role that the area played.

I was told stories about Tsuji, about how the establishment of the red-light district was what the social conditions at the time demanded; about how it was established in the days of Haneji Chōshū,[23] the regent known for his austerity; about how the famous statesman Sai On recognized [the red-light district's] necessity; as well as about how the banquets in Tsuji were called *kugē*, and how warriors of good standing would go to them. I do not know whether or not this had any influence, but in the nineteenth year of the Shōwa era [1944], when I returned home to undergo a physical examination for conscription, Mr. Taira had assumed an administrative position for Tsujimachi's public market.

Although it was a very long time ago, I once met a gentleman who had been a former pupil of Old-man Gichin's when he was teaching at a school in Naha.

Old-man Gichin traveled to Tokyo in either the eleventh or twelfth year of the Taishō era[24] [1922 or 1923]. Therefore, the former pupil was of quite an advanced age at the time. He said, "Teacher was bad at Japanese. "[25]

As an example, he said that Old-man Gichin, issuing a rebuke, had said, "If you keep dawdling, I'm going to throw you!" He had translated the local expression *channagīn* directly into Japanese, but had meant to say, "If you keep dawdling, I'm going to leave you behind!" Realizing what a serious affair it would be to be thrown by their teacher, a warrior, the misbehaving children promptly proceeded apace.

In another episode, Old-man Gichin, who was writing something down in a notebook, was asked by one of his pupils what he was writing. He replied, "I've taken a few things." Instead of saying "taken down," he had abbreviated his response.

It appeared to some people, like the former pupil, that because his teacher was poor at speaking Japanese, he likely experienced difficulties in Tokyo.

That is not something that I know about. But, soon

after arriving in Tokyo, he began friendly relations with such first-rate individuals as the judo master Jigoro Kano,[26] and kendo instructor Hakudō Nakayama,[27] which leads me to believe that he was quite capable of [speaking] Japanese.

I was not in frequent contact with Old-man Gichin, and the time [we spent together] was limited. But I take pride in the many things that I learned [from him]. I appreciate simply having had the pleasure of spending time with him, for which I will always be grateful.

                                  Gisho Funakoshi

NOTES

1 Daruma in Japanese. A legendary Indian monk credited with the establishment of the Zen (Chan) sect of Buddhism.
2 Xhionger Shan in Chinese.
3 Literally "Shaolin Temple Style."
4 The term *kempo* (拳法), literally "method of the fist," is commonly used in Japanese to refer to Chinese martial arts.
5 Azato Yasutsune (1827–1906), an Okinawan karate master and one of Gichin Funakoshi's two principal karate instructors, the other being Itosu Yasutsune.
6 Kunitaro Kosugi (1881–1964), a Japanese artist who began his career as a Western-style oil painter, later taking up traditional Japanese-style ink painting. Adopted the pseudonyms Misei in 1897 and Hoan in 1923.
7 Born Shigeyuki Koda (1867–1947), Japanese novelist and essayist recognized within Japanese literary history for his idealistic writing style.
8 Empire of the Great Ming, the ruling dynasty of China from 1368 to 1644.
9 Ming-era writer who lived from 1567–1624, author of *Investigations on the Five Categories of Things*.
10 Modern Okinawa.
11 1596–1615.
12 The Satsuma domain, or Satsuma *han*, a feudal province controlled by the powerful Shimazu clan.

13 Also Kūshankū. Often described as a special envoy from China during the Ming dynasty.
14 Kōsōkun is believed to have arrived in Ryūkyū in 1756.
15 The former capital of Ryūkyū.
16 Tokugawa Ieyasu (1543–1616), founder and first shogun of the Tokugawa shogunate, the last shogunate in Japan, which ruled from 1603 to 1867.
17 Traditional Japanese footwear, usually wooden-soled and fastened to the foot by a thong that passes between the first and second toes.
18 Itosu Yasutsune (1831–1915), an Okinawan karate master and one of Gichin Funakoshi's two principal karate instructors, the other being Azato Yasutsune.
19 Matsumura Sokon (ca. 1800–ca. 1890), recognized as one of Okinawa's original karate masters.
20 Itō Hirobumi (1841–1909), a Japanese statesman who became the first prime minister of Japan and went on to serve a total of four terms (non-consecutive) in the position.
21 満 means: fullness, sufficiency.
22 寸 is a traditional Japanese unit of length, measuring slightly more than 3 centimeters, or almost 1.2 inches. Here it conveys the meaning of a short distance or small quantity.
23 越 means: cross, exceed, faraway.
24 1926–89.
25 Yamaoka Tesshu (1836–88), born Ono Tetsutaro, founder of the Itto Shoden Muto-ryu school of Japanese swordsmanship.
26 Funakoshi is referring here to two Japanese proverbs. The first is 実る稲穂は頭垂れる (*Minoru inaho wa kōbe tareru*), which, translated literally, means "The ears of rice plants that bear the most fruit hang lowest." Figuratively, the proverb means "The nobler the man, the humbler his manner." The second is 浅瀬に仇波 (*Asase ni adanami*), a direct translation of which yields "Rough waves in shallow waters." In English, the proverb often used to convey the same sentiment is "Empty vessels make the most noise."

27 Often translated as "forms," karate kata are pre-arranged series of offensive and defensive techniques that are performed individually against imaginary opponents.
28 1911–25.
29 In his book *Karate-Dō Kyōhan*, Funakoshi refers to three large scrolls he prepared for the exhibition containing the history of karate and illustrations of kata and techniques.
30 Jigoro Kano (1860–1938), founder of the Japanese martial art of judo.
31 A former location of the Kodokan, the institute established by Jigoro Kano for the teaching and development of judo.
32 Yashitsugu Yamashita (1865-1935). He became the first tenth-dan of Kodokan. The rank was awarded posthumously.
33 Family name of the famous sword master who taught the Tokugawa shogun.
34 The only sword master in Japanese history to become a daimyō (lord).
35 気 refers to spiritual energy, feeling, vigor, mood, etc.
36 In this instance, 正 refers to yang, or positive energy. Additionally, while not mentioned here, a third component of this concept is *fu* (負), which represents negative energy.
37 Keiki Harishige (1885–1952), newspaper and magazine editor and accomplished amateur tennis player.
38 1887–1973, Japanese sculptor and Western-style oil painter.
39 Now the University of Tokyo.
40 Gigo Funakoshi (1906–45).
41 短命 in Japanese.
42 武士短命 in Japanese.
43 Funakoshi here uses the term *bujikara* (武力) for strength, a direct translation of which means "military-arts strength."
44 Written 恋人, using the characters for romantic love and person.
45 As this essay appeared in 1935, Japan's emperor at the time was Emperor Shōwa, also known as Hirohito, who reigned from 1926 untill his passing in 1989.

46 活人剣 (*katsujin-ken*) in Japanese. The concept of a life-giving sword takes into consideration the ways in which a sword can be used—although it can be used to take a life, it can also be used as a means of benefiting others to save, or "give" life.

Afterword

1. The author here uses the honorific suffix *ō* (翁), meaning old man or venerable, to refer to Gichin Funakoshi. Despite the somewhat irreverent tone of the English translation, it is meant as a show of respect.
2. In the Shuri dialect, *ufudunchi*, written 大殿内, is also used as a term of respect when referring to another's home, as well as to indicate a large or stately residence.
3. Written 思亀, using the characters for think and turtle.
4. Pronounced *gi* and meaning: justice, righteousness, morality, honor, etc.
5. Written 容, using the character for form, shape, figure, etc.
6. The characters the author uses to write Gijin are 宜仁, most likely due to the similarity to the name Gichin.
7. 1926–89.
8. Sai On (1682–1761), an eminent statesman of the Ryūkyū Kingdom and one of the best known figures in Okinawan history.
9. Tei Junsoku (1663–1734), a Confucian scholar and diplomat of the Ryūkyū Kingdom.
10. Heshikiya Chōbin (1700–34), a literary scholar and playwright, recognized as the foremost literary figure in early-modern Ryūkyū.
11. Traditional Japanese footwear, usually wooden-soled and fastened to the foot by a thong that passes between the first and second toes.
12. Written 松濤, using the characters for pine tree and waves; a metaphor suggesting an analogy between the sound of the wind as it passes through pine trees and ocean waves.
13. In 1871, the then relatively new Japanese Meiji government did

away with the traditional feudal domain, or *han*, system and established a prefecture system in its place to facilitate a centralized government authority. In actuality, since Gichin Funakoshi, born in 1868, was only around three years old at the time, it is highly unlikely that he would have been able to offer any first-hand recollections of life before the domains were abolished.
14 *Ganko-tō* (頑固党) in Japanese. A faction in Okinawa that was obstinately opposed to the Meiji government edict banning the traditional topknot hairstyle.
15 Also known as Chifijin, the high priestess of the Ryūkyū Kingdom.
16 King Shō Kei (1700–51), who reigned from 1712 to 1751, was the 13th king of the Ryūkyū Kingdom's second Shō (尚) Dynasty.
17 Kumejima is an island located approximately 100 kilometers (just over 62 miles) west of Naha, which shared close ties with China during the time of the Ryūkyū Kingdom.
18 The Ryūkyū islands were not considered to be part of the Japanese state until 1879, when Japan claimed sovereignty over the kingdom and renamed the region Okinawa prefecture. Following the end of World War II in 1945, Okinawa was occupied by the United States and under control of the U.S. military until 1972, when the U.S. government returned administrative authority to Japan.
19 King Shō Tai (1843–1901), who reigned from 1848 to 1879, was the 19th and final king of the Ryūkyū Kingdom's second Shō (尚) Dynasty.
20 Born Shinken Maezato (1897–1970).
21 In Gunma prefecture, approximately 120 kilometers (75 miles) northwest of Tokyo.
22 Tsuji Town, another reference to the Tsuji red-light district.
23 1617–75. Also known as Shō Shōken. A Ryūkyūan political reformer who served as regent, second in authority only to the king, from 1666 to 1673.
24 1912–26.

25 The native dialect of Okinawa differs significantly from the Japanese language spoken throughout the rest of Japan, hence the reference here to "Japanese" (*Yamato-guchi* [大和口] in the original text).
26 Jigoro Kano (1860–1938). Founder of the Japanese martial art of judo.
27 Hakudō Nakayama (1873–1958). Founder of modern *iaidō* (commonly translated as "the art of drawing the Japanese sword") and the only martial artist to attain master instructor status in the three sword-related martial arts of kendo, iaidō and jōdō.

(英文版) 空手道の神髄　The Essence of Karate

2010年4月26日　第1刷発行

著　者　　船越義珍
発行者　　廣田浩二
発行所　　講談社インターナショナル株式会社
　　　　　〒112-8652　東京都文京区音羽 1-17-14
　　　　　電話　03-3944-6493（編集部）
　　　　　　　　03-3944-6492（マーケティング部・業務部）
　　　　　ホームページ　www.kodansha-intl.com
印刷・製本所　大日本印刷株式会社

落丁本、乱丁本は購入書店名を明記のうえ、講談社インターナショナル業務部宛にお送りください。送料小社負担にてお取替えいたします。なお、この本についてのお問い合わせは、編集部宛にお願いいたします。本書の無断複写（コピー）は著作権法上での例外を除き、禁じられています。

定価はカバーに表示してあります。

Printed in Japan
ISBN 978-4-7700-3118-1